SPAIN

AND PORTUGAL:

Democratic Beginnings

edited by GRANT S. McCLELLAN
Editor, *Current Magazine*

THE REFERENCE SHELF

Volume 50 Number 5

THE H. W. WILSON COMPANY

New York 1978

THE REFERENCE SHELF

The books in this series contain reprints of articles, excerpts from books, and addresses on current issues and social trends in the United States and other countries. There are six separately bound numbers in each volume, all of which are generally published in the same calendar year. One number is a collection of recent speeches; each of the others is devoted to a single subject and gives background information and discussion from various points of view, concluding with a comprehensive bibliography. Books in the series may be purchased individually or on subscription.

Library of Congress Cataloging in Publicaton Data

Main entry under title:

Spain and Portugal.

    (The Reference shelf ; v. 50, no. 5)
    Bibliography: p.
    1. Spain—History—1975–   —Addresses, essays, lectures. 2. Portugal—History—1974– —Addresses, essays, lectures. 3. Spain—Foreign relations—1975–   —Addresses, essays, lectures. 4. Portugal—Foreign relations—1974– —Addresses, essays, lectures. I. McClellan, Grant S. II. Series.
DP272.S63   946.083   78-11298
ISBN 0-8242-0626-6

PRINTED IN THE UNITED STATES OF AMERICA

12-11.78

PREFACE

Spain and Portugal, having only recently shed their years of dictatorship, are now launched on the all-consuming and seriously difficult task of pursuing their separate democratic beginnings. As a result, Iberia today is being closely watched as the two nations take the steps that many hope will bring democracy to fruition politically, economically, and culturally.

It is with these three phases of development in the two countries—political, economic, and cultural—that this compilation is chiefly concerned, although other areas are touched on, including foreign relations.

Change has come rapidly in the last few years in both Spain and Portugal. Necessarily, therefore, the articles in this volume are of very recent date. Even so subsequent developments may well outdate some conclusions set forth here, especially in the economic realm. Informed observers now take grimmer views than recently about the two nations' abilities to achieve and maintain an economic stability in which the new democratic structures can flourish.

Section I of the compilation gives an overall view of the political transformation of the infant democracy in Spain, and subsequent sections deal with the many challenges to its existence. The present economic crisis, aggravated by worldwide economic conditions, is examined in Section II, and the evolving culture that has brought about a new permissiveness is discussed in Section III. Regional differences and unrest, beginning to surface, are pinpointed in Section IV. Section V is devoted to all aspects of Portugal's political, economic, and cultural struggle to survive as a democratic member of the world community.

The final section, on the foreign relations of both Spain and Portugal, describes those international organizations that might nurture and sustain the new governments in their struggle to succeed.

The editor wishes to thank the authors and publishers of the selections that follow for permission to reprint them in this compilation.

GRANT S. MCCLELLAN

October 1978

CONTENTS

VI. IBERIA AND FOREIGN RELATIONS

The Iberian Peninsula (adapted by permission)

I. THE CHANGE IN SPAIN

EDITOR'S INTRODUCTION

Spain's political development since the death in 1975 of dictator Francisco Franco has been both sudden and wide-ranging. How the changes have affected the political life of the nation—and the entire fabric of the traditionally conservative Spanish society—is the subject of the first three articles, by John Midgley, a contributing editor of *The Economist* magazine, Horace Sutton, editorial director of the *Saturday Review*, and Stanley G. Payne, professor of history at the University of Wisconsin.

Enlightened leaders, free elections, and a democratic constitution in the making have all appeared on the scene. But perhaps the single greatest political change is the appearance of political parties of the Left, espousing points of view and philosophies made illegal by Franco after he overthrew the Spanish republic in 1937. For the first time in four decades, Communists and Socialists are legal, vociferous, and represent a considerable base of political power. The last four articles in this section, all dealing with the Spanish Left, are written by Constantine Menges, Stanley Meisler, Temma Kaplan and Jon Wiener, and from *The Economist*.

SPAIN'S YEAR OF WONDERS [1]

When the official television network in Spain devoted six hours of viewing time to the far-flung celebrations of the Hispanic version of Columbus Day (Día de la Hispanidad) on October 12, 1977, bored viewers wrote irritated letters to the editors of newspapers, and their complaints were pub-

[1] From article by John Midgley, contributing editor of *The Economist*. *Harper's Magazine*. 256:23-4. F. '78. Copyright © 1978 by *Harper's Magazine*. All rights reserved. Reprinted from the February 1978 issue by special permission.

lished: a far cry from two years ago, when the chance of publication would have been assessed at zero and the letters would not have been written. Getting the tedium, the solemn triviality, and the official obsequiousness out of the television programs will take a little longer.

While the Spanish press has caught on to its new duties and new opportunities with astonishing speed and is suddenly as good as any in Europe, the electronic media find it harder to change to new ways. Nor are political leaders naturally good at steering such a process. In Spain the government has agreed that its control of television, never yet diluted since television began, be shared with the opposition parties, and so the problem of television as a threat to political liberty is being solved. How to convert television from a self-serving bureaucracy into a service to the viewers is another question again. If you look around the domain of public institutions you see the question multiplied a hundredfold.

None of the clichés about Spain will stand up anymore. The first to go is the notion of a country deeply wrapped in ritual conservatism. The reverse side of that coin is the belief, equally long-established, that when not held firmly in their places by monarch or dictator or priest the Spaniards are hopelessly factious, incapable of compromise or toleration, unpredictably violent, and generally ungovernable. Plenty of historical episodes can be cited in support of each of these complementary views. That same history is reflected in Spain's contributions to the language of politics, which consist mainly of words like *junta, caudillo, cacique, pronunciamiento*, and *guerrilla*. In the early nineteenth century the Spaniards did, however, contribute another word, "liberal," which soon entered into the politics of most of Europe and eventually, with its sense considerably changed, into those of the United States.

Spain at that time enjoyed a moral respect in Europe that most of the European states did not, because of the national uprising against French conquest that began in Madrid on May 2, 1808 (the horrors of which Goya so powerfully portrayed in his drawings). Napoleon was baffled by it because it happened nowhere else. The Spanish rebels were not following any particular political theory, but their spontaneous action did oblige their intellectual class to produce a theory of politics that could work independently of the old monarchy and outside the French empire. They produced a theory of eighteenth-century enlightenment liberated from eighteenth-century despotism.

Free Elections After 41 Years

None of this did Spain much good, as things turned out, but the Spanish turbulence between 1808 and 1840 was a pioneering process that contributed fertile elements to the political life of nineteenth-century Europe. That was the end of that, for practical purposes, until 1977. Last year, once again, Spain appeared to be showing others the way. Spain had its first free elections in 41 years last June and made a popular happening out of them. Quite undeterred by the sad, uncertain, divided scene that the European democracies present at the moment, the Spanish people decided to join them and did so with enthusiasm and style. Elderly widows in black stood close to peer at the fine print of the campaign posters. Motorcades blaring announcements and scattering leaflets for one party or the other occasionally encountered each other in the streets, but instead of scowls or abuse there were jokes, and each group would solemnly offer the other its campaign literature. Party chiefs attacked each other with the utmost courtesy. Old linguistic imports, fallen into disuse under the long reign of Franco, took on a new life. A party chief is a *lider*, the rally that he addresses is a *mitin*. *Lideres* showed spectacular agility in getting to *mitines* from one end of the country to the other. By tacit agreement they harped little on the Francoist past, dwelling instead on the dawn of a new day. For the most part they offered philosophy, instead of programs, giving the voters the chance, just this once, to vote not on immediate issues but on what they believed in. A rare piece of luck for any electorate.

This may have been wise of the *lideres*, for when the great electoral happening was over, the new day dawned on an appalling array of national difficulties and problems. Wages and salaries had been allowed to rise merrily in the easygoing months before the elections. Price inflation was accelerating. In August it reached three percent for the month, and with the best efforts of Suárez's government and all the labor-union cooperation he could reasonably hope for, the increase of consumer prices in 1977 most likely turned out less . . . than 30 percent. Industrial activity has been low and unemployment well over 10 percent. Spain's energy problem is at least as bad as that of any European country, and the energy deficit in its balance of payments is $5 billion a year, a huge figure for the weak Spanish economy and the inelastic Spanish foreign trade to carry. Industrial investment was at a standstill; confidence both in the peseta and in the industrial outlook having shrunk to nothing, the money that was not leaving the country was going into real estate, the value of which was shooting up. In various parts of the country agriculture was in an uproar about high materials costs and low product prices. There was general agreement that the budget deficit had to be reduced, but none about the measures—spending restraints, tax increases, or price increases by the nationalized industries—by which this might be done.

Spanish Voters Pick Adolfo Suárez

The voters on June 15 did not hold it against Adolfo Suárez that his government had done nothing about any of these things. Nobody had offered them any reason to suppose that another government would have done any better. They gave Suárez a working majority in the Congress, the chamber of the Cortes that was designed to reflect the popular will directly. They gave the traditional Socialist party with its bright young leader, Felipe González, next place, with a huge lead over any other single party. They rebuffed on the one hand the conservative Popular Alliance, which sought the Francoist vote and stressed "continuity" and order in its propaganda, and on the other hand, the Communist, who, however, got what they wanted: admission to open political life as a recognized party in a democratic system.

The curious thing about Mr. Suárez was that he had, strictly speaking, no party at all, but owed his leading position in Spanish politics to the choice of the young king, Don Juan Carlos. Juan Carlos had been picked by Franco in his declining years expressly to continue the regime; of course he did nothing of the kind. Franco died in November 1975. Six months later the king chose as his prime minister (known in Spain as "president of the government") Suárez, a fairly obscure functionary of the Franco regime, not known at all as either a leader or a champion of reform, to whom he gave the task of effecting the transition from the old regime to a new system of representative government.

If Adolfo Suárez did little else in his first 18 months, he did that job well, miraculously persuading the old unrepresentative Cortes to permit a revival of party politics, authorize democratic elections, and vote itself out of existence, while the king kept the army calm and gave the necessary air of authority and continuity to the vast change. Suárez then presented himself to the voters at the head of a miscellaneous coalition of "liberals," Spanish style, moderate conservatives, and other centrists.

Spain has no monarchist majority and probably no centrist majority either, but the people realized that the kind of changes the king and Suárez offered had to come first, before the bread-and-butter problems of national policy could be fought over. They were the country's best bet for effecting the transition to a modern, Western-European system of government without upheavals and violent attempts to put the clock back. The other party leaders were on the whole not reluctant to accept this result. Santiago Carrillo and his Communist party got a disappointingly small vote, but it was Carrillo who praised Suárez: "Intelligent, well-intentioned, and not a prisoner of the past," said Carrillo—and before the election, at that. In November he said it again: "A patriotic Spaniard and a good democrat."

In that general spirit, many excellent opportunities for

censure and recrimination were ignored when the new government devalued the peseta (three weeks after the election and six months later than it should have) and declared that the gravity and urgency of the country's economic difficulties required immediate national attention. The parties, Socialists and Communists included, were willing to cooperate in administering to the sick economy a stiff dose of orthodox economic medicine. Suárez resisted the many calls for a government of national union and continued to stand on his Center coalition, but he put together a cabinet chiefly of bureaucrats like himself, men from the departments, from the state industries, from the higher government inspectorates, with a sprinkling of eminence in the universities and of experience in the private banks.

By October they had prepared the outline of a new economic policy designed to slow inflation down to an annual rate of 10 percent by 1979, restrain demand at home, and, thus, revive the interest of Spanish producers in selling their products for export and increase the tax revenue. The labor unions were asked to accept restraint in their wage demands, beginning at a level of 22 percent in the first year and going down as price inflation diminished. Since, following the abolition of Franco's unitary labor-organization system, the revived labor-union groups are competing ferociously among themselves for members, this was not an easy demand to accept, but the leaders, at least, accepted it. The employers' associations pulled a long face. On top of being asked for price restraint, they are threatened with reform of a tax system that has been a paradise of loopholes. Most singular is the fact that after two days of discussion government and opposition parties agreed to support this program.

In sum, government by consensus prevails. There is general agreement to give parliamentary government a chance. A thousand terrible rows lie in wait about the things that politics from day to day are about: power failures, school textbooks, water quality, housing, street paving and lighting, hospital services, form-filling, police methods, bus services, and of course money in every context. They cry for attention, but they have to come next.

SPAIN'S NEW DEMOCRACY [2]

These are grave and uncertain days at Moncloa, the elegant little palace with its tall cypresses, its spreading evergreens, and its gravel walks that is home and command post for the Spanish prime minister. The double iron gates are closed, and the names of those who come to visit are checked off by a covey of civil guards who stand at the portal with patent leather tricornered hat, rifle slung over shoulder, a walking memoir of days that were bitter and fierce. It is as if in the village a certain sadness had come to the family in the big house on the hill and the seigneur suffers deep travail.

Moncloa's marbled halls, paved with deep carpets, stalked always by ushers and secretaries, have been the domain of Adolfo Suárez, the 44-year-old centrist, a favorite of Juan Carlos, king of Spain, who with his Greek queen lives nearby in the Palacio de la Zarzuela.

The king and Suárez, whatever their prior political cant, are now avowed democrats who, each domiciled a few miles from the hunting lodge at El Pardo where Franco lived, must endure the shadow of El Pardo and that of its former tenant, His Excellency, the Chief of State and Generalissimo of the Armed Forces, Don Francisco Franco Bahamonde, Caudillo of Spain, the onetime general of Spain's African army who, by circumstance, became führer and duce and stayed to rule the nation absolutely and in archaic trappings over four decades.

Together now, king and prime minister must thread Spain through minefields and trip wires of the most explosive political and social topography surveyed since the summer of 1936, when, after one malevolent turn upon

[2] From "Democracy in Spain: can the impossible dream come true?" by Horace Sutton, editorial director. *Saturday Review*. 5:10-14+. O. 29, '77. ©
Saturday Review, 1977. All rights reserved.

another, the fledgling republic dropped into the pit of a civil war that left at least half a million dead and scars upon the living and upon the nation that will be carried into the next millennium.

There are those who suggest that the setting in Spain now is, ominously, as it was in 1936. By that they mean that the army and the wealthy classes were aligned on the far Right, the Socialists were the largest single party, and the economy, then as now, was shaky.

Eroded now is that euphoric edge so evident in the spring of 1977, when the Spanish people went to the polls for the first time in 41 years, discarding the repressive reign, voting a middle-of-the-road coalition ticket, but awarding more than 28 percent of the popular vote to the Socialist Workers party, a radical version of Willy Brandt's socialism. Indeed, Brandt's party had backed its Spanish counterpart, led by Felipe González, a 35-year-old lawyer exuding a boyish charm who made his party the largest in Spain.

Dimmed, perhaps, is the noble purposefulness that welled out of the first meeting of the elected Cortes addressed by the king. Now the autumn is here, and the leaves fall on a restive nation where inflationary winds stir discontent. The rich, beclouded by a paranoia of tax fear, equate the imposition of levies with Communism; and workers threaten a season hectored by strikes.

These are the nettles that can attend democracy, unknown in a nation of novitiates who, babes in the woodlands of freedom, fear to pick benign mushrooms lest they prove to be buds of anarchy. It is a curious and unfortunate circumstance of the times that the Spanish people have at last been able to turn to democracy only to find they have done so at the very moment when the sheikhs have plunged the world into an oil-fueled inflation.

In the best of the Franco years—whatever the loss of liberties—Spain was racking up a comfortable balance of payments. By 1973 it had developed the largest tourist industry in the world. The 35 million foreign visitors who came that year outnumbered the population by a million.

The editors of the Michelin guide to Spain likened the economic importance of Spanish tourism to the value of Peru to the kingdom in the sixteenth century.

Moreover, upwards of a million workers had found their way to the far side of the Pyrenees and, working abroad, were sending back earnings that amounted to a sum so sizable it became Spain's largest earner of foreign currency after tourism and manufactured goods.

In the blooming of prosperity, Spain, so long so poor, so long the holes-in-the-knees cousin in the boondocks beyond the mountains, became a consumer society. In 1960 four Spanish families out of a hundred had refrigerators, and four out of a hundred had cars. Now 88 out of a hundred have refrigerators, and every second family has a car. On a sunny weekend the road from Barcelona to the seaside retreat of Sitges becomes so jammed with cars that those who leave after ten o'clock of a Sunday morning stand little chance of getting back before midnight.

In the last years of the Franco reign—he died in November 1975—the oil crisis derailed the Spanish express. Tourism, so bountiful a gift, especially in areas once considered arid and useless, fell off sharply, leaving the resorts with empty hotels and lonely beaches. Workers laid off abroad returned home seeking jobs. Franco moved to pacify the workers, granting them raises of 20 and 30 percent a year; but that only puffed the cheeks of inflation even more.

It was against that economic landscape that the Franco years ground at last to an end, and Juan Carlos as king moved to establish a constitutional monarchy. When it came time to vote, it was strange to comprehend that only those who were 64 or older had ever before cast a ballot in a free election. Seventy percent of the nation is under 40; they had lived all their lives under the strict lacings of the absolutist Franco regime. Yet the country took no collective chances—it neither ratified Franco's far Right nor did it depart archly from it by moving far left; it went right down the middle.

To dismantle the fascist government, Spain turned to

new leaders, many of whom had been workers in Franco's party. Perhaps only such a group, retaining some credibility with the Right because of their Franco connection, would have been capable of such an artful job of field-stripping the fascist mechanism without sparking an explosion on the Right. The army has traditionally preferred a central government, and in the rightest view, anarchy always lies bubbling just below the surface. Take the lid off the pot, even a bit, and you can't put it back on, they said. And while the rightest Alianza Popular, headed by Manuel Fraga Iribarne, former minister of the interior and onetime ambassador to the Court of St. James, picked up an anemic 8.2 percent of the popular vote, the guns rest in reactionary hands. The crack army division Brunete Number 1, named after a famed civil war battle, remains in tether just north of Madrid.

In the delicate balance on which Spain teeters, the army is contained by Juan Carlos, a monarch as popular in the barracks as he is in the yachting circles of Majorca. And memories had only to turn back two years to recall a photograph of Adolfo Suárez in blue shirt and white tunic bearing the Falangist clutch of arrows on his shoulder boards. He was then head of the Movimiento Falange, the party that had its origins in a group of young self-anointed elitists who, in the early Thirties, undertook as a crusade to rid Spain of incipient Marxism and liberalism. In Franco Spain, the Falange was the sole party, and in the last days of Franco, Suárez was its principal representative.

Having assumed now the reins of the democracy, Suárez is called not an opportunist but a technician. "His specialty," says Dr. Alberto Aza, chief of the Cabinet, "is maneuvering. He has all sorts of magic formulas." Dr. Aza, bearded, articulate, silky, and just 40, accompanied Suárez on his visit to the States and was so nimble with translations and with the press that he was made aide-de-camp on the spot. Aza's own Franco years, which embraced his entire life, were spent in the diplomatic service in Algeria and in Rome. "One was either a hero living abroad, or in prison, or working in government," he explains. The private sector, to young men for whom political power was catnip, seemed not to have been an alternative.

Spain's Regional Troubles

Suárez, the handsome, telegenic premier, is the handpicked favorite of Juan Carlos, himself handpicked—chosen over his father, Juan, still in exile in France—to be king of Spain. Since the death of Franco, Juan Carlos has behaved like a committed democrat. He is aware that the only way to consolidate the monarchy is to identify it with democracy. His brother-in-law, the former King Constantine of Greece, who comes to sail with Juan Carlos in Majorca, is now selling cars in England.

Monarchist roots do not grow deep in Spain, and royalty does not bask in an aurora borealis of reverence and reputation. The last king, Alfonso XIII, Juan Carlos's grandfather, installed a dictator to rule over the kingdom and finally abandoned the nation in 1931, opening the way for the second republic and, ultimately, the civil war.

Although the Left, which holds a commanding position, will only tolerate the king as a constitutional monarch with no powers to govern, Juan Carlos has made his points. Diplomats skilled in taking political temperatures say that if a referendum on the question of keeping the monarchy were held today, the king would win. As a political chess piece, he is also the guarantor who keeps the military out of politics.

Strange as it may appear to Western democratic sensibilities, it is Suárez, the former Falangist, and Juan Carlos, the king created by General Franco, who have presided over reform. Together with the new bicameral Cortes—a parliament that embraces a crazy quilt of figures including Socialist Felipe González; rightist Manuel Fraga Iribarne; Santiago Carrillo, head of the Communist party; and Dolores Ibarruri, now 81, the storied *la Pasionaria* of civil war days, home from exile in Russia and once again a delegate—they must face the demands for home rule that are pressed by the Catalans and come stridently, and often flooded with terror, from the Basques. The six million Catalans, who occupy a triangle of land with the Pyrenees on one side and the Mediterranean on the other, have often been called the Jews of Spain. With Barcelona as their capital and an array of factories strung out along the coast, the industrious Catalans are responsible for production far beyond their numbers.

In 1936, speaking their own language, flying their own flag, and governing from their own headquarters, the Generalitat in Barcelona, the Catalans bitterly opposed the nationalist coup that brought Franco to power, fought bitterly in the conflict, and were bitterly oppressed when the civil war was done. Franco forbade the Catalan language, banished the flag, and dissolved the Generalitat. Catalan leaders scurried into exile. The emergence of Majorca and the Costa Brava as prime tourist resorts in the 1950s tempered the oppression in those areas.

Because of the Francoist repression, some young Catalans cannot write their language, but today the Catalan tongue is back in full use. On the Ramblas, the mile-long promenade in Barcelona, the kiosks sell Catalan newspapers, each of them sporting the Catalan flag in color. A Barcelona teenager, come to take Sunday lunch at Pá i Trago, a bistro that features Catalan dishes, wears blue jeans with a Jesus label, drinks Coke, and carries a handbag affixed with a sticker that glows with the Catalan flag and the exhortation *En Català, si us plau*—"Say it in Catalan, please."

Last summer the Catalan leader, Josep Tarradellas, in exile in France since the Franco victory in 1936, returned to Spain to confer with Adolfo Suárez. Now, with the return of the Generalitat, home rule seems at last a certainty, but the problem may prove more sticky than that. Catalonia is pushing for commercial autonomy as well, to ensure that its tax money is not funneled away to industrialize Madrid.

The Basques, who occupy provinces in the north of Spain, along the Pyrenees and the Bay of Biscay, caught the separatist revival fever from the Catalans early in the century. Grown rich and independent on iron, steel, wood, and shipbuilding, and finding their markets outside of Spain, the Basques were filled with the *machismo* of independence, a life apart from Spain. Those heady dreams brought them frightful suffering in the civil war, but it failed to cool the fever. One of Franco's last acts was to condemn to death young Basque terrorists who, in the spirit of separatism, had taken to assassinating policemen. Last June, Basques kidnapped a Bilbao industrialist and killed him when his family declined to meet a ransom demand of nearly $6 million.

In the heat of summer, the Basques demonstrated violently, especially in the resort at San Sebastián, choking the streets with barricades and smashing windows in banks and shops. The police replied with smoke grenades, nightsticks, and rubber bullets.

The Cortes is studying the idea of eliminating the Guardia Civil and Los Grisas, the grays, from Basque provinces and giving local government its own police responsibility. But there are those who believe that police and civil guard must be retrained to consider themselves protectors of the people rather than an extension of the government, free to violate the people's rights in pursuit of their version of law enforcement.

The police and the civil guard have traditionally been run by seconded army officers. But, as Hugh Thomas writes about them in his epic tome *The Spanish Civil War*, "with their green uniforms, three-cornered hats, their Mauser rifles, and gaunt barracks, this police force was regarded as if it were an army of occupation." Its members were taught to remain aloof from villagers, and they never served in the part of Spain from which they came. Their reputation for ruthlessness was not unwarranted, and villagers came to hate them and set upon them with a vengeance when provoked. In *Seven Red Sundays*, Ramón Sender, the novelist, put it this way: "When one joins the civil guard, one declares civil war."

Today the civil guard (whose image some Spaniards try to soften by likening them to Canadian Mounties) is a formidable force of 65,000. Add to that 35,000 grays and the combined paramilitary force grows to 100,000, almost half the size of Spain's standing army. Although there is said to be considerable uncertainty in their own ranks on how they should properly embrace the law, especially after 1,000 of their like went to jail after the coup in Portugal, and although they are considered more tractable than they were a year ago, they continue to inspire as much fear as loathing. "Around here," says a foreign journalist working in Madrid, "you don't go around saying, 'Hey, Jack, what's your shield number?'"

If the government must reeducate the police, it must do as much for the wealthy classes, who have by tradition, almost by code of honor, as it were, avoided paying taxes. "Not paying your taxes is a sport in Spain," says José Ortega Spottorno, the publisher who started Spain's lively new daily, *El País*. Son of the famed philosopher Ortega y Gasset, and a senator appointed to the Cortes by the king, Ortega privately believes that it will be necessary to catch two or three "big fish" in income tax evasion before the workers believe that democracy has truly arrived. "It hasn't happened yet," he says, "but it is fundamental." There are still no criminal sanctions for income tax evasion.

"To Get Out of the Crisis," reads the cover line of a recent issue of *Cambio 16*, Madrid's snappy new weekly magazine, "Let the Rich Pay." But the rich, many of whom have moved bank accounts out of the country, have shown themselves in prior times more willing to risk a political coup than to pay their taxes. In the fearful days of 1936, they looked for a coup to deliver them from reform, but they got instead a civil war of class against class. It was then that they turned to Italy and Germany for help, igniting what Hugh Thomas has called "a world war in miniature."

The reeducation of the rich will have to be aimed at the industrialists of Barcelona, the wealthy families in the Basque north, and the landowners in Andalusia and Estremadura. "Does all this mean I have to have my luggage ready?" an industrialist asked Suárez recently at a reception attended by the king. Said Suárez, "If you are ready to renounce 50 percent of your privileges, you can stay."

The king, overhearing the conversation, turned to Suárez after the man had left and said, "Don't you think you've been too hard on him?" And then he added reflectively, "Well, it's not bad that they sample the air."

The New Democratic Permissiveness

The air dances with freedoms, or rather, democratic permissiveness. In a nation that lived under ultrapuritanical strictures during 40 *franquista* years, a nation where the church's laws were the government's laws, the changes are dizzying even to the visitors who have lived in the democratic West. Kiosks once as sober as the library in a nunnery are festooned with pornographia, not quite as hard core yet as the displays on Scandinavian and American newsstands, but in Spain they seem as startling as a nude in church. An enormous billboard on the Plaza de Callao, heralding a film called *Homo Eroticus*, with Ira von Furstenberg, shows a doctor examining a naked male. The viewer sees only the patient's back, but the doctor's wide-eyed expression and the direction of his gaze are clearly saying, "I have never seen anything like *that* before."

Nightclubs along tourist row offer dancers nude except for shoes. A play about an aging philanderer who finds revitalization with a young girl has a scene in which the girl, fondled by her lover, romps bare-breasted on the bed. The Madrid version of *Equus* has left in the nude scene that brought gasps from the Wednesday matinee-goers when the show first opened on Broadway.

"In France," says publisher Ricardo Utrilla, who lived abroad for many years, "workers save. In Spain we are trying to live fast and well. Forty years without life has made Spaniards eager to live."

Sometimes the lust for life has spilled over into the ludicrous. Last summer the self-styled Commandos of the Love War for Moral Democracy, describing themselves as a militant lovers group, were asking for the right to make love in public. Only a year ago policemen were cautioning young couples strolling with arms about each other's waists against exhibiting displays of affection in public.

In the *franquista* time a billboard showing a girl's bare shoulder brought an outraged call from the wife of the minister of information and tourism. Any autocrat in or out of government could take private censorial action. Someone close to a government official could influence a television commercial. Young and Rubicam's Charles Alexander recalls situations where a housewife in a commercial might appear too real, not properly up-scale. "A helpful nudge to the right people would suggest that the commercial was not 'giving the image of the Spanish people we would like to convey.' No more was needed to take it off the air."

Decisions were arbitrary. A book series on the history of the civil war was allowed to be sold but could not be advertised. A manufacturer of sanitary napkins could advertise the name of the product but could not show it in an advertisement or say what it was for.

Now, advertising agencies seem to vie with one another in producing suggestive ads. A manufacturer of bathing suits is promoting his product with a simple advertisement showing a couple swimming nude in clear water. Each is holding aloft a bathing suit recently doffed. Says the copy, "It is a beautiful thing to swim without a bathing suit, but if you have to have one, buy ours."

A celebrated ad for Wrangler jeans shows a bare-chested man. Female fingers, nails bright with polish, are undoing the snaps on his jeans. The top button is already open. Says the caption, "Wrangler can resist if you can." "In the old days," says Alexander, whose firm handles the rival product, "we might have had trouble trying to describe Levi's curve and fit."

Sniffing the air and finding it salubrious for its product, *Playboy* is considering a Spanish edition. Why not? The market is certainly ripe. An enterprising money-maker who paid 10 million pesetas for the home viewing rights to an eight-millimeter version of the film *Emmanuelle* with a black cast is selling 3,000 prints a week.

Strangely enough, the same censorship commission that acted so harshly before is still in office and is still headed by Jaime de Urzaiz, director general of advertising activities. In the new liberalism there are certain restrictions on health claims, and if advertisers say "better" or "more" they must prove it. But the moral code has dissolved.

Such an abrupt turn of the compass heading has left some officials as dizzy and confused as are some senior citizens after all those years entrenched in authoritarian, puritanical *franquista* dogma. An upper echelon minister, having lunch with Ricardo Utrilla not long ago, leaned across the table and said, "Look, you know all about democracy and all I know is Francoism. On this matter we have discussed— is this decision Francoist or democratic?"

Still on the books is a 1966 press law, written by the rightist leader Manuel Fraga Iribarne, that says it is illegal to criticize the army, the king, or the unity of the state. It was quietly relaxed, especially after the king delivered a pro-reform speech before the US Congress during his American visit in the spring of 1976. During that trip *Cambio 16* printed a cartoon depicting the king dancing across a star-studded New York skyline. The king was not offended, but government rightists were, and they demanded that *Cambio 16* be suspended for four months. That brought outcries from *El Pais* on one hand (which called a four-month suspension "an indefinite suspension of the credibility of reform") to the *Washington Star*, on another, which in an editorial on June 17, 1976—the election was still a year away—wrote: "Conservative elements in Madrid have got to learn that a free press is not just the luxury of a society already free but something of special value to a society trying to choose its own future in an atmosphere of openness and consensus." It called the freedom of *Cambio 16* "a profoundly significant test of the intentions and good faith of the new government in Madrid."

The king intervened and *Cambio 16* was free, but not off the hook. A year later Fraga got a court order to seize copies of *Diario 16*, *Cambio's* hard-hitting daily. Carlos Arias Navarro, the ex-prime minister whose resignation *Cambio* had called for (and who was ultimately sacked by the king before the elections), started court proceedings because of a satirical article about him in *Diario 16*.

In America, William Buckley's *National Review* ran an article by British writer Robert Moss that praised Fraga, warned of Soviet plots to destabilize Spain, and called Ricardo Utrilla "an active Communist party member." No Communist, Utrilla, who had been a correspondent in Washington for the French press, has received death threats and has been followed ominously by car and by motorcycle. He was finally placed under police protection. This summer, bombs were set off in the printing plant of *Diario 16*, near the Eurotel. Fortunately the building it occupies was built for heavy industry, otherwise it would have collapsed. But the German presses, valued at more than $250,000, were wrecked. The 34-year-old editor, Miguel Aguilar, believes it to be the work of Grapo, a secret group of agents provocateurs whose purpose is to stir terrorist action that will wreck the democracy and bring in the army. A firm believer in Adolfo Suárez, Aguilar says, "The press has played an important role in the sunrise of Spanish society."

The Limits on Women's Rights

At times, press freedoms have become entangled in the archaic laws that limit women's rights. An article about birth control published in *El País* last February brought that paper a fine of 200,000 pesetas. Spanish laws dealing with women date from the nineteenth century, and since Franco made church laws into national laws, abortion and divorce are illegal. The law prohibits the use and sale of birth control materials and the promulgation of information about them.

Divorces in the form of church annulments have been obtained by actors and prominent people, but they are unavailable for the rest of society. Women send to London for intrauterine devices and then seek out young liberal doctors to insert them. Prescriptions are needed for birth control pills, but older doctors are loath to write them. For abortions, women call a number in London. The respondent answers in Spanish and advises the date of the next abortion flight. The cost, less than that in Paris, includes pickup at the airport.

Until the laws are rewritten, Spain remains no woman's land. Without need of witnesses, a husband may accuse his wife of adultery. If the case is proven to the satisfaction of the court, she is liable to a six-year jail term. But a wife needs witnesses even if she knows her husband maintains a mistress in a separate apartment, and to prove him an adulterer she must prove that her husband slept with another woman in the family home.

All this is a fertile field for women's rights leaders. Pilar de Yzaguirre, a pert, fiery mother of five, formed the Association for Promotion and Cultural Evolution as an underground society two years before Franco died. It was legalized in February of 1975 and maintains headquarters in a poster-covered flat in a Madrid apartment house. Under a printed fanfare that shouts, "si si si, dolores a madrid," a Communist exhortation, and the American contribution that shows a woman standing with men along a row of urinals, Yzaguirre and her deputies send out literature and plan their speaking tours. But so ingrained in Spanish culture is the fabric of *machismo* that women to whom the basic principles of women's lib are explained just laugh.

A cultivated Madrid matron, a working mother who listened to Yzaguirre said later, "It has become chic to glorify Dolores and to cast her as a symbol of women's rights. I don't hold to that. She sent too many people to their death to claim the right to emerge now as a social heroine." At dinner one night, the wife of an upper-middle-class industrialist, well traveled, well educated, and well off, held forth spiritedly about the inequities that exist in women's rights. "The new democracy will change all that," she said determinedly. But then her face darkened and she added. "But I am afraid, really afraid, of all those Communists. They could take over."

The Communist Party Legalized

The Communist party was legalized in Spain in what is now considered a masterstroke of political legerdemain engineered by Suárez and Juan Carlos in the quiet of the Easter holidays, while militant minds were turned toward more reverential directions.

"Never, never in my life," said the young daughter of a retired Francoist general who had served in the Canaries, "had I ever seen my father so angry. I thought he would explode when he heard the news." But the fury evidenced itself only with the resignation of the admiral heading the naval ministry and with some rightist demonstrations that were a counterattack to the spirited street celebrations in the workers' sections of Madrid.

Santiago Carrillo, who was the 20-year-old secretary general of the United Socialist Youth in 1936, reentered post-Franco Spain as head of the Communist party. But Carrillo returned as a Eurocommunist, the author of *Eurocommunism and the State*, a book having a lively sale in Madrid bookstores. In its criticisms of the Kremlin in matters ranging from human rights to failure to dissolve Stalinism, the book has provoked the ire of the Soviet high command, which would like to unhorse Carrillo and replace him with one of the party faithful along the lines of Soviet purist Alvaro Cunhal in Portugal. Only Ceaucescu of Romania, among the leaders of the Soviet bloc, came to Carrillo's defense, but in Spain Carrillo's position is firm. Having seen the nation suffer from 40 years of oppression, Spanish Communists, like Spaniards of other political persuasions, are inclined to be sharply critical of the Soviet record in matters of human rights.

Rid at last of the oppressive far Right, the nation is not likely to move to the far Left unless severe worker unrest further unbalances the economy. The autumn could indeed bring a rash of strikes, but a coalition of Suárez's party and that of González, called for in some quarters, seems unlikely.

Spain's Foreign Relations

Spain is eager to convince Scandinavians, the Teutons of the north, and the Dutch that it is a democratic country and no longer a European outcast. Getting in the Common Market would award it a tacit seal of approval from other nations and provide it with better markets for Spanish agriculture and industry. In the larger view, the Common Market is a step toward an eventual united Europe that could be socialist with an assortment of leaders to choose from—Mitterand, Brandt, Schmidt, González, or Soares.

Although the Spanish military would like to be a part of the professionalism of their Western European counterparts and the democratic center is in favor of joining NATO, Socialists and Communists are opposed. The Socialists see the 1953 treaty that gave the United States bases in Spain as a move that served to entrench Franco in power. The embrace, so well photographed, between Eisenhower and Franco, was symbolic to the Spanish Left—and dispiriting. Spaniards who opposed fascism had held out postwar hopes that once Germany and Italy had been vanquished, the Allies would turn on Franco.

The American base at Torrejon, the air base at Zaragoza, the standby base at Morón, and the naval station at Rota may bolster the Spanish economy, but to the Spanish Left they are holdovers from the cold war and an extension of the United States and the imperialist aims it has exhibited in Central and South America. Moreover, in the likelihood that US bases in Central Europe are overrun, Spain would be the natural fallback arena of operations.

For its part, Spain, sitting behind the wall of the Pyrenees, seems less disposed to consider a threat from the east as it is watchful of one from Africa, where every warm zephyr crossing the narrow straits, only 36 miles wide, could carry whisperings of trouble. Already Radio Free Canarias broadcasts with impunity from a station inside Algeria. And if an unfriendly African nation, Algeria or Morocco, say, were to make a move toward the Canaries, who then would protect Spain's interests?

To add foreign affairs to the ledger of problems facing a new old nation beset with uncountable domestic conundrums seems basely unfair.

The Role of Youth

The real hope of this ancient consortium of clans, which as an imperial power dispatched Columbus on his voyage of discovery of the New World, Magellan on his circumnavigation of the globe, and the conquistadores on the conquering missions that left the Iberian imprint from California clear to Tierra del Fuego, is its youth. It is a youth born, weaned, and reared on pure fascism—and that has emerged into maturity as democratic. "To be young is to be a democrat," says an influential journalist in Madrid. The average age of the editors of *El País*, already Spain's second largest newspaper, is 31. Its editor is 32. His opposite number on the rival *Diario 16* is 34. Of the key politicians, Suárez, the centrist, is 44; González, the putative socialist heir apparent, is 35. The king, in a pivotal role, is 40. Even the church, so influential a voice in the chaotic days that led to the civil war, and so powerful a partner in the Francoist 40 years, is strangely silent. Not until the 1960s did the church begin to withdraw from its relationship with Franco. Young priests would not accept the church's political involvement and its participation in a political constitution. Today young worker-priests stand for election on the Communist ticket.

The church and the *franquistas* will shudder when the Cortes, as it surely will be, is asked to consider a divorce law and relaxation of abortion laws, along with equal rights for women, home rule for Catalans and Basques, and municipal elections. Many young people are convinced that the only solution for Spain is a federal state along the lines of the American system, with the central government collecting taxes, allocating public works, and assuming responsibility for defense and foreign affairs. The concept crosses party lines and finds as much favor with Socialists as it does with centrists.

"Democracy Has Begun"

On a scorching sunlit day last July, Juan Carlos, dressed in the full uniform of the commander-in-chief, crossed under the awning of the Cortes, just up the block from the Palace Hotel, to address the first elected parliament of the new Spain. A year and a half had passed since he had delivered his first message as king, and the Spanish world at that time had shuddered, heaved, and begun to turn again in a direction that had been considered inconceivable a few months before.

The monarch stood at a lectern and surveyed the circle of delegates—Suárez, the pragmatist, dapper, artful, handsome; Fraga, pompous Francoist who gives out books filled with colored pictures of himself in various fancy dress, including that of ambassador to Britain; Carrillo, the youth leader who had lived and aged a lifetime during 40 years of exile and had come home to lead the Communists; Ibarruri, *la Pasionaria* (of whom the rightists once claimed that she had severed the throat of a priest with her teeth), back after 38 years in the Soviet Union; Felipe González, the boyish Socialist; editor José Ortega, son of the philosopher-intellectual José Ortega y Gasset, at 60 once again a motivating journalistic force as originator of *El País*, and legislator as well.

"Your presence in this room" Juan Carlos told them, "the representations that each of you claims; the plurality of ideology . . . demonstrate . . . the desire for national harmony . . . and the recognition of the Spanish people's sovereignty."

To achieve a national harmony, the king said, "we had to address as a guarantee of the exercise of all liberties, the demands of the evolution that arose from the development of our culture, the change of generation, and the material growth of the present times." To achieve this, it was he who was to propose that everyone participate in political life.

"The law makes us all equal. But what is important is that no one feel marginal." He called for a constitution, for justice in human relations, for the exercise of authority with restraint, for the creation of vehicles to insure the dignity of man.

And then, finally, the phrase came. In his splendid uniform with the solitary row of gold buttons running down the dark tunic and a modest array of ribbons on his chest, the king surveyed the chamber, all the remnants of Franco, the Communists who had survived the exile, the reactionaries who had become democrats, the youthful Socialists—and to the polyglot group, this young man, ordained by a repressive, archly conservative army commander to be king of all Spain, uttered the absolute words. "Democracy has begun."

That was Friday, July 22. On the prior Sunday, a pale reed of a man, Protasio Montalvo, the former Socialist mayor of the town of Cercedilla, emerged from the hiding place where he had lived, in fear of his life, for 38 years. "My ambition is to live a few more years," he declared. Protasio Montalvo knew, too, that democracy had at last arrived in the kingdom beyond the Pyrenees.

THE POLITICAL TRANSFORMATION OF SPAIN [3]

Most observers agree that the political transformation that occurred in Spain after the death of General Franco in November 1975 is impressive and in some respects breathtaking. It constitutes a political transformation without any clear parallel or analogy in twentieth-century systems: an established, institutionalized authoritarian system (not merely an ad hoc Hispanic military dictatorship) has been totally liberalized and transformed from the inside out by means of the personnel, institutions and mechanism of the regime itself, starting with the Head of State. The only

[3] Article by Stanley G. Payne, professor of history, University of Wisconsin, whose latest book is *Basque Nationalism. Current History.* 73:165-8+. N. '77. Copyright © 1977, by Current History, Inc. Reprinted with permission.

analogy that has been mentioned, Turkey after [Kemal] Atatürk [founder of the Turkish Republic], does not bear comparison, because the Turkish republic was conceived as the first twentieth-century expression of guided democracy within a third world mold. Nor is the recent Portuguese revolution similar, either, because the Portuguese dictatorship suffered the standard fate of institutionalized modern European authoritarian systems: it was overthrown by forces stemming from foreign (in this case, colonial) affairs. Post-Franquist Spain remains a unique example of voluntary, pacific internal transformation.

This is the more ironic in view of Generalissimo Francisco Franco's firm determination to avoid "the Primo de Rivera error" of failing to institutionalize his regime so that it could survive him. [Primo de Rivera was dictator of Spain from 1923 to 1930.—Ed.] Why was Franco's 40-year regime so easily dismantled? In fact, the question should be reversed; Franco's major achievement was that he kept his system largely intact until his own death. Moral issues aside, the basic weakness in the historic-political position of Franquism lay in the fact that the "third force" national authoritarian systems lost World War II in Europe. When Franco came to power he was riding the wave of the future; in the Europe of 1939 there were more mixed authoritarian states than liberal democratic or Communist countries. After 1945, Franco became a dinosaur.

Contrary to the common view of Franco's "reactionary" regime, the Franquist government always intended to promote economic and social modernization. Franco has recently been derided for having assumed that he could keep Spanish society unchanged, but this was never his intention. What was crucial for Spain was that the industrialization and urbanization of Spanish society in the 1960s and 1970s took place within the cultural and social context of secular, materialist, socially democratic West Europe, conditioned by mass tourism and more international experience than the Spanish people had ever known. As a result, the regime lost out in the minds and hearts of most Spanish people, even though the same people (or their parents) would have supported the regime under different circumstances several decades earlier.

Franco spent most of his career as dictator adjusting to circumstances he could not control. If he made a major personal political mistake, it was his choice of a successor. Juan Carlos, the present King and the grandson of Alfonso XIII, the last King (1902–1931), was brought to Spain by Franco in 1953 because he was the only logical and legitimate way to solve the succession problem. The conversion of the dictatorship into a regency in 1947 stabilized the regime and provided legitimacy by recognizing the historic institution of the monarchy as Spain's legal form of government. After 1943, Don Juan (father of Juan Carlos and the then heir and pretender) had adopted as his program a European-style parliamentary monarchy and had promised to dismantle the entire Franquist system. For this reason, Franco bypassed the heir-apparent in favor of his son, hoping to educate a young and impressionable prince in the values of the Franquist regime.

Juan Carlos played his role with such effectiveness and discretion that he was officially designated as Franco's successor and the next King of Spain in 1969. Careful never to overstep himself during Franco's lifetime, he nonetheless indicated his own political values during the early 1970s. Even before the death of Franco, it seemed likely that Juan Carlos as King would prove more his father's son than Franco's obedient pupil.

By the time that Franco finally died in November 1975, the stage was set for drastic change. Franco had not been foolish or shortsighted enough to suppose that Juan Carlos —or any other royal successor—might not tinker with his system or try to reform it. He planned to circumvent such a contingency by an elaborate constitutional structure of corporative and oligarchical institutions, with the proviso that the incumbent Prime Minister was not to change automatically with the installation of a new Head of State. If Franco's closest political collaborator, Prime Minister Carrero Blanco, had not been assassinated in December 1973, he would have remained in office as guarantor of the regime's continuity for as long as two years after Franco's death. Thus Carrero's spectacular murder by terrorists belonging to ETA (a Basque nationalist group) was a crucial development in Spain's political evolution, tellingly directed against the future of the regime. Carrero's successor as Prime Minister during 1973–1976 was Carlos Arias Navarro, a weaker and less effective figure, who lacked Carrero's ability to rally the old guard against change.

The Crucial Period

The first eleven months of the transition, from November 1975 to October 1976, were crucial to liberalization. The dismantling of the regime's authoritarian institutions might have occasioned a fatal backlash from the entrenched right and the military; instead, reform was successfully accelerated in 1976. Juan Carlos initially made no effort to remove Arias as Prime Minister despite his pro forma resignation immediately after Franco's death. Arias's temporary continuation seemed necessary to reassure the "bunker"—as Franquist diehards were labeled by the opposition—during the early transition. Moreover, in 1974–1975, Arias himself had made a few feeble gestures toward reform; by the beginning of 1976, he was charged with their acceleration, particularly in the direction of civil rights and political representation. Juan Carlos made it clear at the outset that his role was not to manipulate the daily workings of government. Yet he expected action from Arias's new ministry, whose most notable members were two former Franquist luminaries, José Maria de Areilza, Foreign Minister, and Manuel Fraga Iribarne, Minister of the Interior. Areilza, particularly, set the tone of reform during the first half of 1976, promising fundamental liberalization and constitutional revision within a brief period.

The new Arias government expanded civil rights and liberalized controls, but it made little progress toward the most basic reforms, especially in the realm of political structure, above all because Arias did not have his heart in it. By July 1976, Juan Carlos felt sufficiently sure of himself to move more rapidly and asked Arias's resignation. The military indicated they had no desire to intervene in the legal conduct of a government able to govern effectively and legitimately. Arias went quietly and was replaced by Juan Carlos's personal selection, the 43-year-old bureaucrat and politician Adolfo Suárez González.

The first reaction to the appointment of this relatively unknown figure was anguish among liberals and reformists who greeted Suárez's appointment with cries of "Adolfo who?" Suárez, in fact, had served in minor political and administrative posts during the last 15 years of the old regime and had come to Juan Carlos's personal attention as the national director of Spanish television. He first attained Cabinet rank in the second Arias ministry formed after the death of Franco, when he served briefly as minister for the Movimiento (the old Falangist state party).

Although he was a product of the Franco regime, Suárez had matured during its last pseudo-liberal phase and had no illusions about its viability or the importance of bringing Spain into line with the rest of Western Europe. He was not a core Franquist but a politician of the younger generation, the generation that official propagandists had for some time —and with greater accuracy than they dreamed—been referring to as the *generación del Principle,* that is, of Prince Juan Carlos. The new monarch had accurately gauged Suárez's flexibility, political tact, and talent for personal relations.

By the summer of 1976, it was increasingly evident that the Franquist minority in Spain was largely impotent without Franco. The official Movimiento was demobilized, and popular support was lacking. Once the power of the state was placed behind the process of de-Franquization, the only institution that might have interfered was the armed forces.

The Military

One of Juan Carlos's major contributions to democratization was his tactful management of the Spanish military.

This proved to be an easier task than had been anticipated, because the Franco regime had itself promoted the de-politicization of the military. Although the dictatorship maintained a special relationship with senior commanders, army officers were in general encouraged to concentrate on professional matters and to leave governing to the government. By 1976, most of the Spanish officer corps belonged to the post-Civil War generation. Although they were moderately nationalist and politically conservative, they were conditioned by the climate of the 1960s and 1970s. Many of them expected, and nearly all accepted, Spain's growing adaptation to West European political and social norms. In addition, the dictatorship had astutely prevented the formation of cliques or concentrations of power among army commanders, so there was no strong leader or cohesive group within the military that could easily initiate a new praetorian course. Finally, throughout modern Spanish history elements of the military have intervened in politics only during periods of uncertain legitimacy or incipient breakdown, when the established government seemed unable to govern. Neither of those conditions obtained in Spain during 1976. There were persistent murmurings among small factions of ultras, but no serious threat ever materialized.

The King's private lunches with top commanders and a series of personal inspections and reviews held the respect of the army command and helped to maintain institutional loyalty throughout the transition. When the Vice President of government for national security, the right-wing General Fernández de Santiago, was forced to resign in September 1976, he was replaced by Lieutenant General Gutiérrez Mellado, the outstanding liberal among senior commanders. Gutiérrez Mellado kept the military in line politically, while preparing for a series of structural and technical changes that would lower the overall age of command and improve the army's military efficiency. A special meeting between the new Prime Minister and ranking lieutenant generals and admirals in September 1976 produced an expression of support for the reform policy, except for a verbal veto of the legalization of the Spanish Communist party. Early retirement of a number of key ultra-right commanders was also effected.

The way was then clear in October 1976 for the most crucial single step, the Law for the Reform of the Cortes (Parliament), which replaced the authoritarian corporative system of Franco with a directly elected democratic Parliament of two chambers, an Assembly and a Senate, the only limitation being that approximately 18 percent of the Senators were to be designated personally by the Crown. The most remarkable fact about this reform was that for the most part it was not strongly contested by the old Franquist deputies. Whereas in the summer of 1940 the democratically elected Parliament of the French Third Republic voted itself out of existence in favor of an authoritarian Pétainist regime, the opposite occurred in Madrid in the autumn of 1976: an authoritarian, corporative Parliament voted itself out of existence in favor of a democratic Parliament based on free parties and elections, even though most of the old deputies who voted in favor of the reform stood little chance of being elected by a democratic party system. With Franco dead and the tide running so strongly against them, most Franquists accepted defeat.

Suárez was ably assisted by the speaker of the Cortes, the flexible regime veteran Torcuato Fernández de Miranda, and the new Minister of the Interior, Martin Villa, who adroitly administered the sometimes severe problems of internal order created by kidnappings and political murders by a variety of left and right extremist groups. Throughout the fall and winter of 1976–1977, the reform government coolly refused to allow itself to be provoked by outrages from small bands of either extreme, while pursuing its program of legal and institutional reforms. The police were placed under new leadership, their policies were altered and their activities were curbed. Full civil rights were restored and, by the early spring of 1977, all political parties had been legalized except for a few tiny left-wing terrorist groups.

The only problem was the main Spanish Communist

party (PCE) itself. (There are, in fact, a dozen or so Spanish Communist parties, all more or less at odds with the regular PCE.) Spain is the only Western country except Cuba to have lived, briefly and only in part, under a government in which the Communist party played a hegemonic role (Juan Negrin's Spanish People's Republic of 1937–1939). The brutality and intolerance of the Communists during the Civil War led most sectors of the Spanish left to adopt a virulent anti-communism by the time that the Civil War ended. During the 1960s, however, under the leadership of Santiago Carrillo, the PCE swung strongly toward what has since become known as "Eurocommunism" and the tactics of parliamentary democracy.

Although the PCE retains the concept of "democratic centralism" and a system of internal authoritarianism, it has gone even further than the Italian Communists in espousing external democratic principles. By 1977, it seemed on the verge of an open break with the Soviet Union. Conversely, there was a widespread belief among liberal and leftist opinion in Spain, and in West Europe as a whole, that the democratization of Spain could not be genuine and complete unless the Communists were legalized as well. The government officially legalized the PCE in April 1977 incurring only relatively mild protest from the military; soon afterward, Spain's first democratic parliamentary elections since 1936 were scheduled for June 15.

Competing Political Organizations

Although political organizations had been forming and reforming themselves ever since the death of Franco (producing a total of more than 200 so-called "parties" by 1977), serious mobilization in most cases did not get under way until a few months before the elections. By the time that contest was announced, it had become clear that there would be five or six main contenders. Small extremist groups, neo-Franquist, neo-Falangist or the terrorist revolutionary left, could be easily discounted, because the new parliamentary reform established a list system of voting for provinces and large urban districts that favored broader parties and alliances. The main force on the parliamentary right was the Popular Alliance, a union led by seven former Franquist ministers (chief among them Fraga Iribarne) devoted to a kind of reformist Franquism that would save as much as possible of the old regime.

More moderate and nearer the center was a new coalition called the Democratic Center, formed in September 1976 under the aegis of Areilza and Pio Cabanillas (a former Franquist Minister of Information), which planned to vie for the broad centrist vote of the Spanish middle classes. After the elections were announced, Suárez himself decided to join forces with this confederation, now reconstituted as the Union of the Democratic Center (UDC), unofficially under his leadership.

Since the small Social Democratic groups had been unable to organize an effective party of their own—some of their elements choosing to join the UDC—the only other centrist forces were the equally divided Christian Democratic groups, which finally formed a coalition, "Equipo" ("Team"). The democratization of Spain, however, occurred too late for a Christian Democrat victory. By the 1970s, Spanish society was becoming more strongly secularized and the kind of appeal that proved effective in Italy in 1946 had scant resonance in Spain. Combined with the weak leadership and the internal bickering of the Spanish Christian Democrats, this lack of appeal resulted in their virtual annihilation in the elections.

The Left was divided into three different sectors: Socialist, Communist and the multiparty regionalist groupings. There are altogether about threescore Socialist parties in Spain, but the only one that counts is the main-line Socialist Workers party (PSOE), the direct descendant of Spain's original Second International Marxist Socialist party, first officially organized in 1888. The history of the PSOE is marked by persistent ambivalence between revolutionary Marxism and social democratic reformism. In 1931, the PSOE was the largest single political force in Spain, only to lose that position to political Catholicism and then veer toward what Socialist radicals called "Bolshevization," thus playing a major role in provoking the Civil War. During the long opposition to the Franco regime, the Socialists often played second fiddle to the well-organized, well-financed Communists. The latter, however, were for long little more than a Soviet party in Spain, whereas the Socialists sustained their tradition as the main organized political voice of Spanish collectivism.

Reorganized in 1972 under vigorous and somewhat radical young leadership, the Socialists became extremely active after the death of Franco and mounted a very intensive electoral campaign, partly financed by West German and Venezuelan money. Though the PSOE leadership has officially defined the party as a "Socialist, not a social democratic, party," their electoral campaign was effectively ambiguous, in the best tradition of this ambivalent organization. The young secretary general, Felipe González, projected a very attractive image as the energetic leader of a potentially radical but not irresponsible leftist opposition to the new liberal monarchy.

The outcome of the voting on June 15, 1977, was a disappointment for the extreme Left and the extreme Right, a total disaster for the Christian Democrat coalition and a major victory for the moderate Right and moderate Left. With official support and the backing of national television, Suárez's UDC came in first, with 34 percent of the popular vote and 47 percent of the parliamentary seats, thanks to the majority list voting system. The big surprise winners were the Socialists, who won 29 percent of the popular vote —far more than they won in 1931 or 1936—and benefited from the structure of the voting system to the extent of garnering nearly 34 percent of the parliamentary seats.

By contrast, the showing of the Communists, who won 9.2 percent of the vote and 5.7 percent of the seats, was decidedly poor, far below the 15 percent polled by Stalinist Communists in neighboring Portugal. Given the opportunity to vote for a strong non-Communist left, many blue-collar Spanish workers refused their support to Communists. Initially, the Eurocommunist tactic had been a relative failure, and in some quarters memories of the PCE's Stalinist past remained too vivid. The right-wing Popular Alliance was even less successful than the Communists, winning eight percent of the vote and 4.6 percent of the seats.

The other surprises in the elections were the relative weakness and the moderation of the regionalist vote. A moderate coalition of liberal Catalanists won only 10 seats in Catalonia compared with 15 for the Socialists and nine for the Communists. Similarly, in the Basque country, the largest Basque nationalist party, the historic PNV, only tied the Socialists, with eight seats apiece. In Galicia, home of the third largest regionalist movement, the elections were largely swept by Suárez's UDC and the same was true in the Canary Islands, focus of Spain's latest regionalist movement, where several months earlier terrorism had been indirectly responsible for the deaths of nearly 600 people.

Since the overall results were comparatively moderate, disturbances were relatively slight and satisfaction was expressed about the fairness of the balloting and tabulation—though not exactly of the entire electoral system—the outcome was hailed in Spain and throughout the Western world as a great victory for democracy. In the immediate sense, this was undoubtedly correct, but the broader question of the future remained.

The relative victory of the UDC was a political victory for Suárez (and for Juan Carlos). Though the UDC fell short of a parliamentary majority, it was easily able to form an alliance with small centrist groups to provide the votes that enable the government to have a chance of completing a full parliamentary term until 1981. The Socialist (and general leftist) claim that the 1977 elections should be considered elections for a constituent assembly, not a full-term Parliament, have been rejected. The Socialists themselves accepted no such argument when they were part of a victorious constituent coalition in 1931, and there was no reason for their rivals to accept different logic in 1977.

Whether the new Suárez parliamentary government can rule successfully for a full four years is another matter. Work on a formal new constitution will soon have to be completed, and the most important single remaining reform is some kind of measure for partial autonomy for Catalonia and the Basque country—and perhaps extension for other regions as well—that should be presented to Parliament during 1978.

Economic Problems

Aside from the regional question, the major domestic political issues of the late 1970s will be economic. Understandably, the first reform governments of Juan Carlos concentrated on political and institutional questions almost to the exclusion of pressing economic matters. As a result, the Spanish economy already suffering the effects of the 1973 West European recession, sank into severe stagflation during 1976. Industrial employment declined; production sagged; the balance of payments deficit reached alarming proportions; and by the time that elections were held in June 1977, the annual rate of inflation was nearing 30 percent, worse even than Italy and Portugal. Industrial labor had taken advantage of the new freedom to force major wage and benefit increases, pushing up labor costs at least 27 percent in 1976, and management found it hard to take a firm stand to keep costs in balance.

There was widespread talk in government and in management of the need for a "social pact" and a new austerity program to promote the recovery of the once-booming Spanish economy, but the government postponed unpopular decisions until after the elections. In the second Suárez Cabinet formed in July 1977, a new vice presidency of government in charge of economic affairs was created for the respected economist Enrique Fuentes Quintana, who has the difficult task of directing the new austerity program and coordinating the other economic ministries. He introduced major features of the new policies in a national television address in mid-July. Most dramatic was an immediate 25 percent devaluation of the peseta, but this was to be followed by stringent new wage guidelines accompanied by business incentives and a further liberalization of long-standing financial restrictions. In keeping with the current economic programs of France, Italy and Portugal, the main target was inflation, not unemployment, but the program was sweetened for workers by prominent emphasis on a major progressive tax reform (for the first time in half a century) and extensive improvements in unemployment and social security benefits, to be administered by an expanded and much more heavily financed central state system.

The initial response of labor and leftist party spokesmen was not entirely clear. Many had been taking a hard line, pledging no social pact or economic agreement that did not include further wage increases for the lower paid sectors, new employment stimuli and more extensive measures of state socialization. However, Spanish labor, as in the past, does not speak with a single voice. The old state syndical system was dissolved in the spring of 1977, but it has been replaced by multiple and competing labor organizations, first of all by the Socialist UGT and the Communist-dominated Worker Commissions (CCOO). Such rivalry can lead to increasingly extreme positions, but in fact the first response to the government seemed relatively conciliatory.

A Slender Margin

The UDC plurality over the Socialists was less than five and one-half percent of the total vote, a slender margin easily subject to erosion, especially because the UDC is not a firmly organized and unified party but a loose coalition of small groups and notables that Suárez will have somehow to weld into a cohesive organization. Its lead in the 1977 elections was due in part to the genuine centrism and moderation of the Spanish middle classes but also in large measure to Suárez's special prestige for having led the democratization, bolstered by the authority of established government. Whether these advantages can be sustained in the face of the increasingly unpopular decisions that the Spanish government will soon have to take is at best a moot point. The next confrontation will occur when the first municipal elections are held, presumably in October 1977. The Socialists will enjoy a formidable position in most of the larger cities, but they are currently riding the crest of a somewhat ambiguous opposition role. When they have to assume more direct responsibility, the Socialists too may encounter problems of party unity and new mobilization.

It has been observed that the major Spanish political transitions of the twentieth century occur in the worst possible economic settings. The advent of the Second Republic coincided with the trough of the Great Depression and the general collapse of parliamentary government in southern Europe, while the almost completed democratization of the new monarchy has taken place in the wake of the major stagflation of the 1970s rather than in the great boom of the 1960s. Democratization has been carried out with not inconsiderable political skill, to which the overwhelming majority of Spaniards have responded with prudence and moderation, belying their supposed "unpolitical temperament."

Nonetheless, the structure of the new Spanish system has not yet taken complete form, and the party system itself is still in evolution. The relative insulation of Spain from foreign influence is ended, and the effects of any drastic changes or leftward swings in Italy or France will be strongly felt. Nearly all sectors of Spanish politics accept "Europeanization" and most Spaniards are eager for membership in the European Community, but in military matters nearly all the Spanish left is overtly or covertly neutralist. Like their neighbors in Lisbon, the current Spanish leaders are expecting further major assistance from the United States and possibly from the European Community to see them through their current economic difficulties; while on the other hand the Soviet Union has greatly expanded its own interest and activities in Spain.

The moderation manifest both by the government and by most Spanish people during the transition was no sham. Comparatively few Spaniards seek drastic change, but many want an improvement of their slowly deteriorating economic condition, a problem that will provide the immediate battleground for Spanish politics during the next few years.

RIGHT AND LEFT VS. CENTER IN SPAIN [4]

Two years ago, with the death of General Franco, 36 years of dictatorship came to an end in Spain. The effective leadership of King Juan Carlos, the tactical skills of Prime MinisterAdolfo Suárez, and the cooperation of most political and economic groups have since brought about peaceful transition to free elections and a functioning democratic government. Spaniards have had a sense of satisfaction with the dramatic political changes they have accomplished.

Now, however, this calm and optimism are being replaced by another mood, a mood of fear, one that people try to push away, like a nightmare to be forgotten. I talked last fall with political leaders of the center, the Left, and the Right, with Communist, Democratic Socialist, and anarchist labor union leaders, with modern and traditional businessmen and bankers. All saw shadows of an earlier failure of democracy, in 1936, and they gave whisper to their fears. From every political direction the same lament: Why did fate have to choose this time for Spain to try to make democracy work? Spaniards remember vividly that the military dictatorship of the prosperous 1920s came to *its* end just as the world depression was starting. Then too the transition from dictatorship had been welcome and peaceful during the first two years. The elections of 1931 were organized by a reform coalition much like the group that brought about the free elections in 1977. And on both occasions the Spanish people voted overwhelmingly for the parties of the center. Nevertheless, after the first elections in the 1930s the economy kept getting worse, labor unrest

[4] From "Deepening Shadows Over a Fragile Democracy," by Constantine C. Menges, who has written a report on Spain for the Center for Strategic and International Studies, Georgetown University, Washington, D.C. *Worldview.* 21:14-18. Ap. '78. © Copyright 1978 Council on Religion and International Affairs. Reprinted with permission.

grew, terrorism intensified, and the culmination of pressures broke the unity of the center political parties. From there it was a steady, agonizing slide downward while the economy failed and the democratic center was torn apart by the extreme Left and Right.

"That was 1936. It can't happen again. Spain has changed. This is a modern economy, where most people live at the European standard," they say . . . and hope, and pray. Yes, there is a new, prosperous, economically successful Spain. The elegant streets of Madrid, the bustling cafés and restaurants, the explosion of sensual and political expression, and the traffic jams and new apartment houses are tangible expressions of the good living conditions enjoyed by most people. But stroll along the attractive boulevards to any subway station, walk down the stairs, and take a look underneath the calm surface. The clenched fist holding a machine gun celebrating the Revolutionary and Patriotic Anti-Fascist Front is one among hundreds of terrorist group posters covering the walls. "No to Cooperation With the Government Economic Program," assert posters and speakers representing the big unions, as well as the smaller extremist unions and political parties. Various separatist groups demand "Autonomy for Catalonia!" or for the Basques or for Andalusia. From the Right come the demands of the Carlists, the old Falange, and the New Force, which proclaim the need for "Fatherland, Order and Justice," not democratic political competition. Everywhere in Spain off the main streets these posters, speakers, and causes are visible—from big, bustling industrial cities to small towns on the barren central plain to the newly well-off resort and condominium towns along the sunny coasts. Again and again two words echo—"Amnesty" and "Solidarity." Amnesty is demanded for terrorists, for people arrested in violent demonstrations and marches. Solidarity is pledged for the striking workers in the hotels, transportation, the hospitals, for mailmen, construction workers; the list is long and grows. All of these images may fade away into dim memory, or they may leap from the posters to tear the fragile new democracy to shreds. That is the growing fear.

Three Severe Problems

The next months will determine whether the new democratic system can cope with three severe problems now facing Spain: *first*, the deepening and nearly desperate economic crisis; *second*, the impending deterioration of government services that directly affect many people, such as health care, social insurance, and education; and *third*, the challenge of steady violence from the Right and Left political extremes and from separatist groups, coupled with the tangible power of the extreme Right to change the government. More and more Spaniards from all points on the political compass feel that the government and leaders of the two center political parties are not behaving as though they fully understand the extent of the danger posed by these three problems: the full depth of the economic crisis, the new crisis in government services, and the belief that today no group, right or left, could change the democratic political rules by violence.

Throughout the initial stages of the transition from the Franco system the new political leadership moved in unspoken fear of intervention from the extreme Right. Paradoxically this very sense of danger may have provided the incentives for political moderation that helped assure the great success already achieved. It was also important that any reckoning with a continually deteriorating economy was postponed until the June 1977 national elections provided a firm base for action. As a result, Spain has paid a heavy economic price for its social peace, for it was bought with steady wage increases that kept wages moving faster than the 80 percent inflation of the last three years.

By the fall of 1977 both these elements promoting stability had changed. No longer did the political parties, except the Communists, fear the prospect of violent intervention from the Right. Further, there was consensus on the urgent need to repair the economy. In late October 1977 after several months of shuttle diplomacy among the Right,

center, and Left, Prime Minister Suárez was able to negotiate a comprehensive austerity plan, which was publicly
supported, endorsed, and signed by the four major political
parties. But little else has happened since then, except that
the quiet deterioration of the economy continues; Right,
Left, and regional terrorists groups continue to murder;
and public opinion polls reveal that the current government
has declined sharply in popular approval.

The Current Economic Crisis

The overall and visible dimensions of the economic crisis
can be sketched quickly. After fifteen years of growth, full
employment, and rising living standards, the 1974 world
recession ended economic growth in Spain, led to rising unemployment (now more than one million, or 11 percent of
the labor force), and increased inflation at a rate double
that of the Common Market, reaching 30 percent in 1977.
At the same time, the number of strikes jumped from 3,200
in 1975 to more than 40,000 in 1976, with a proportionate
rise in lost production time. The rate of business failure
has increased steadily, new investment has stopped, and the
balance of foreign trade has turned sharply against Spain.

But private talks with business and labor leaders point
to a situation even worse than these well-known facts describe. Just as inflation has been increasing costs enormously
since the change of regime, productivity has declined markedly. One corporate president said: "I don't need a declared
strike because my employees are on strike all the time. One
out of four comes to work only two or three days a week,
another large group signs in for six or seven friends, and
everybody is working less since they know I can't do a thing
about it." The head of a manufacturing concern told me his
equipment is the same as that used in Germany, but "the
same job that takes one hour in Germany requires eight
hours in my factory." The Franco labor code, still in force,
effectively prevents any worker from being fired once on the
permanent payroll. That, in combination with the high
social insurance costs and the business pessimism, has acted

to limit severely the willingness of government and private companies to enter into "a marriage for life" with any new employees.

More serious still is the fact that thousands of large and small companies are on the brink of bankruptcy because they lack cash to cover current expenses. For years easy financing and tradition have meant that Spanish firms used credit to cover a much higher proportion of their day-to-day expenses than is the usual case in Europe. This was done by using short-term revolving bank credits and by paying suppliers with notes convertible to cash in 30 to 60 days. As part of the fight against inflation the government has cut back on credit, banks are curtailing loans and calling in those that fall due. The shortage of credit meant that, beginning early in 1977, Spanish companies were using 90 and 180-day notes to pay their bills. Because the economic situation got worse, 1977 ended with many companies unable to pay off these notes. And the companies that expected to pay *their* bills once these notes became cash were unable to pay their workers and expenses. There is a clear risk of cascading business failures if the last shreds of hope fade away. Right now their morale is so low that many businessmen talk of "giving the factory keys to the government or the workers and getting out."

During a long, and depressing, conversation, an economic advisor to Prime Minister Suárez sketched other problems pointing to the real possibility of an economic crash in the coming months, including the fact that most large companies were no longer paying social security taxes for their employees. Indeed, they are dipping into their social insurance reserve funds to pay current salaries. This process began in the spring of 1977, when one of the largest government-owned companies, broke and unable to pay its employees, received permission to suspend social security payments and use social insurance reserve funds to meet current expenses. Other large government-owned companies, which account for nearly a fourth of Spain's industrial production, promptly did the same; during the last few months they were joined by many private companies, big and small.

This development will accelerate the second and still invisible element of the crisis—the impending deterioration of vitally needed social services. At present the social insurance system has a budget nearly equal to the rest of the government sector. It covers nine out of every ten persons, currently pays pensions to more than four million retired workers, pays unemployment compensation, provides training for skilled jobs, and pays for nearly all health care and social welfare services. During the years of economic growth there was a steady improvement and expansion of social services, but the last four years of recession have meant a doubling of taxes on employers (who provided nearly all the financing), and, in spite of huge budget increases, a steady decline in the real level of services available. The continuing increase in total unemployment compensation payments and the unwillingness of many government and private companies to make their social insurance payments meant the loss of nearly a quarter of the $12 billion budget at the end of 1977. And, since the government is cutting back on total expenditure for 1978, its budget for the present year makes no provisions to cover this deficit.

There is also a great deal of ferment within the huge government bureaucracies as the newly legal labor unions compete for members by encouraging demands for higher salaries and more participation in management. The Communist and more extreme left-militant unions are making special efforts to win over government employees. During November 1977, there were strikes that closed down all hospitals, public works, the postal service, and airports. Because it is widely assumed that the government, unlike private companies, cannot go broke and close down, the pressure for wages higher than the government's anti-inflation guidelines is likely to remain strongest among government workers.

Then there is the normal dislocation and uncertainty accompanying the gradual replacement of the old Franco leadership at the top while all the civil service bureaucrats

remain in place. Understandably the new leaders come to
public service without previous experience. Most of them
sincerely hope to make government work better, but most
of the social service bureaucracies have been closed to scrutiny for decades, and the new executives have barely the
time and energy to get on top of current problems much
less come up with workable ideas for reform.

Together these elements—financial deficits, labor mili-
tancy, and a thin layer of new hopefuls presiding over the
Franco bureaucracy—virtually guarantee a period of turmoil
and decline in the government's social performance. This
in turn will have a negative political effect, adding to the
loss of confidence in democracy already resulting from the
continued downward trend of the economy and the failure to
implement the agreed-upon austerity program. Private opinion polling done for Prime Minister Suárez indicated that
he personally retained a good deal of support but that his
party and government have lost half the people who voted
for them in the national elections. At the same time, the
most extreme left-wing parties gained in support, and this
pattern can only feed the extreme Right and Left, which
have a number of terrorist organizations ready for action.

The Role of Rightists and Leftists

The common belief in Spain today is that the time of
danger from the extreme Right has passed. In the words of
a union leader: "They know they are getting weaker every
day, and if they were going to move they would have done
it already." True, a number of milestones have been passed
since Franco's death, most notably the 1976 referendum, the
legalization of the Communist party, and the 1977 national
elections. But there remains more than a conspiratorial
Right of the old regime; there is also a social base and tradition for a broader "patriotic Right," which might coalesce
if the coming months suggest that democratic government
is unable to protect the standard of living and assure social
peace. Were the economy to crash or sink at a faster rate,
there might well be tacit popular support for some more

limited form of democracy—not a clear-cut military coup, but still a giant step back from the progress made so far, and almost certain to include the suppression of the extremist left-wing parties, perhaps even the Communist party with its powerful labor union. A forecast of this type of right-wing coalition was provided in September 1977 by a secret and mysterious meeting of high-ranking military officers, who are reported to have asked the king to dismiss Prime Minister Suárez, limit the power of the parliament, and establish an interim emergency government for economic recovery.

One month earlier, in August 1977, the more extreme Right may have acted more directly to halt the transition to democracy when some of its members planted the bomb intended to assassinate both the king and the prime minister. Although it is not certain which extremist group was responsible for that plot, it *is* known that two events of January 1977 were intended to spark enough conflict to give the Right an excuse for intervention. In January five Communist lawyers working on behalf of strikers were murdered and, at the same time, a number of high-ranking military officers were temporarily "kidnapped." That effort at "destabilization" failed, but the Guerrillas of Christ the King, the New Force, and other elements of the extreme right-wing network built over decades continue to organize and plan, awaiting the "right conditions" for acting.

On the left the principal Communist party, led by Santiago Carrillo, has a clearly defined strategy for achieving power. It needs democracy "at this time" to expand its power from the strong labor union movement secretly built-up during the last 20 years and reach into public services such as health, education, and provincial government.

Right now the Communists are anxious to become indispensable to Prime Minister Suárez in helping Spain get through the growing economic and social crisis. If the democracy survives the next year or two, and if the military and Right no longer pose a significant threat, then in four to six years the Communist party will use its new sources of visible and invisible power to achieve a dominant voice in Spain's destiny. Today the 62-year-old Carrillo is the smiling, friendly uncle figure of Eurocommunism, who declares that he is "deeply committed to democracy." During the Civil War he was the Communist in charge of the police in Madrid at the same time suspects by the thousands were rounded up and killed in the early morning hours. Since then all the brutality of Stalinism, admitted even by the Communists, and the suppressions in Hungary and Czechoslovakia have not shaken Carrillo's belief in his political religion. There are many in Spain who wonder whether this new Eurocommunist will ever permit real democracy in his tightly controlled party, much less in the nation.

Carrillo's image of moderation is greatly enhanced by a cluster of more impatient Marxist-Leninist-Maoist groups to his left that proclaim the need for social revolution now. Included in this more extreme Left are three Communist parties, one of them strongly pro-Moscow, which compete with Carrillo's party. Most of these parties control labor unions that are trying to expand, and several of these groups have close ties to active terrorist organizations like FRAP (Revolutionary and Anti-Fascist Patriotic Front) and GRAPO (Armed Revolutionary Group for the Workers). Though still small in absolute terms, these extreme Left groups have caused serious problems: They oppose any cooperative efforts to restore the economy, they have encouraged and stimulated strikes by government and factory workers for wage hikes far above the current inflation level, and they are combining forces to form floating "worker assemblies" instead of visible union committees to bargain with employers. Managers who make a deal with a "worker assembly" today are confronted a few weeks later by another "assembly" with new demands and the argument that the previous assembly was not an authentic representative of the workers. Obviously this tactic represents a fusion of Spain's historic anarchism with contemporary revolutionary tactics.

After a long series of political murders in 1976 FRAP

announced that it was changing from armed struggle to popular violence . . . riots, strikes, and demonstrations. The leadership announced the change of tactics by declaring: "We are growing larger and we will continue to be violent." If one adds up the murders of the extreme Left and the Basque terrorist group, twelve people were gunned down during November 1977. Most of the victims were members of the Armed Police or Civil Guard—two national paramilitary police, which, together with the armed forces and the Directorate General of Security (DGS), were the most unpopular elements of the Franco regime. The new democratic government has moved delicately to separate from each other all four power centers of the Right, while still requiring their domestic intelligence capabilities to reduce the threat of terrorism. But such brutal attacks on the police by the Left and separatist groups will only further increase the rightward radicalization of the very individuals who have most to fear should their former victims feel strong enough to take revenge for past actions. Perhaps the terrorists in the speeding limousine who machine-gunned the home of Prime Minister Suárez twice in one recent month only intended a warning. But from which violent direction—right, left, or separatist?

Can the Democratic Center Continue to Rule?

Any one of these three severe problems would challenge the statesmanship and nerve of even the most experienced government and political leaders. Together they are an immense burden. Will the democratic center bear up under such pressures? One hopes so, but recent political moves by Prime Minister Suárez and Felipe González, leader of the Democratic Socialist party, raise questions about their capacity to limit political competition in the interest of the genuine cooperation required by circumstances. With the support and encouragement of King Juan Carlos, Suárez has used his suave good looks, popular appeal, and tactical finesse to keep one step ahead of events. He created the government coalition, the Center Democratic Union (UCD), out of a mélange of small parties, and he is now trying to shape this into a genuine unified political entity. Although Suárez pulled off a political miracle by getting agreement on a program to put the economy back together, he has failed to make a number of tough decisions needed to implement it. And worse, he is losing credibility because the opposition parties, labor, and business leaders are all convinced that his failure to act is explained by simple, short-run concern to maintain his party's hold on the government.

The most damaging failure is the government's unwillingness to set a timetable and procedure for national union elections. These are urgently needed because the Franco labor-management structure has faded away during the last two years. Only a series of valid union elections can select groups to represent the workers and end the wildcat strikes that are partly caused by competition among the unions. Businesses, labor, and the opposition political parties see the delay as an attempt by Suárez to keep his political rivals from getting a firm labor base, for the government party has itself no affiliated union. This erosion of support leaves Suárez and the government with such allies as the loose, still unstable coalition of small parties and the disciplined Communists, just as the economic situation gets worse.

The other half of the political center, the Socialist Workers party (PSOE), has a long history and a young, dynamic leadership committed to democracy and practical reforms. It is by far Spain's largest single political party, winning by itself 34 percent of the seats in the congress, as compared with the slim majority put together by the many coalition parties of the UCD government. After making the important decision to help the government repair the economy by negotiating and signing the austerity program, the Socialist party backed off when it saw the enormous political prestige this conferred on Suárez and his party. It did this by highlighting its role in shaping the final outcome "in the interest of the workers" and by a publicity campaign making it clear that only with the help of the Socialists could the government turn the paper agreement into action. But when the first tests came—a series of strikes by public employees—the Socialist party and its union tried to play it both ways: They supported the strikers' excessively high wage demands . . . based on complex arguments that exempted these strikes from the austerity plan.

At the same time, Felipe González, the 37-year-old, magnetic, handsome, and articulate leader of the Socialists, began to refer to his party as a "serious alternative to power." He proclaimed this not only in Madrid but also during a visit to the United States. At that time the first democratically elected Spanish government since 1936 had been in office barely four months! To some degree this was a sharp reaction to González's perception that Suárez and his government were tilting toward union election procedures to favor the Communist unions, hoping thereby to avoid strengthening the Socialist party as a result of its union becoming the major voice of organized labor. González went on to suggest publicly that if Suárez continued with his efforts to keep the Socialist union from having a fair chance in the union elections, the result might well be a coalition government formed by the Socialists and Communists.

Santiago Carrillo, the Communist leader who remains sober about the threat from the Right, spoke sarcastically about the Socialist position: "Politics," he said, "is for serious people. If Felipe González wants to revive popular fronts, he should go back to Madrid and talk to the Maoists, because we certainly aren't for those luxuries." The realistic Carrillo knows that it is several years too early to cause anxieties on the Right about any type of direct Communist participation in government, and he understood that the rash and premature words of the Socialist leader only served to weaken the willingness of the extreme Right to tolerate Spain's democracy.

Given the fragile nature of the new democracy and the severe economic, social, and political problems facing Spain, the only hope for continued success lies in a democratic center that acts with courage and statesmanship. Prime Min-ister Suárez has demonstrated masterful tactical leadership and the ability to maneuver toward specific goals. Now is the time for him to worry less about keeping his party ahead in the campaigning for the 1978 municipal elections or the 1979 national elections and to do what must be done to hold the economy and society together. He can then count on the results to provide the political approval at the polls. Felipe González and the Socialist party would do well to shift from their current posture of "semiloyal" opposition and coop-erate fully in helping the government to carry out the austerity program. Instead of hoping to reach power as a result of the current government's failure, they can count on their distinctive reform program, traditions, and local poli-tical base to gather voter support in future elections. In the short term continued political bickering within the demo-cratic center that prevents effective government carries great risks of massive social unrest and some type of imposed solution from the Right. Even if the immediate dangers are overcome in the next year or two, failure to take this mo-ment of challenge to firmly establish the traditions of re-sponsible cooperation and loyal opposition is to risk the demoralization and fragmentation of the democratic center, leaving Spain highly vulnerable to the Communist alterna-tive in four to six years. The choice rests squarely with the political leaders and parties of the center in this new democ-racy.

THE STRANGE DEMOCRACY IN SPAIN [5]

In the name of lasting democracy, the government of Premier Adolfo Suárez is running Spain in a way that hardly seems democratic. On critical issues, Suárez prefers to nego-tiate with the opposition in private, bypass the elected par-liament, and issue laws by decree.

[5] From "Democracy in Spain Is Strangely—and Ominously—Undemocratic," by Stanley Meisler, correspondent in Spain. Los Angeles *Times.* p 2 IV. D. 4, '77. Copyright 1977, Los Angeles Times. Los Angeles Times/Washington Post News Service. Reprinted with permission.

The 45-year-old, popular and energetic Suárez recognizes the undemocratic nature of some of his actions but insists they are necessary at this stage of Spanish political development.

A few Spaniards fret over the dangers of this. In a recent editorial, the Madrid newspaper *El País* called the process "administered democracy." But this kind of criticism is rare.

Most Spaniards have no quarrel with these methods of government. The opposition accepts the need for emergency measures at this time. So do most newspaper commentators and editorial writers.

The lack of concern probably stems from two feelings. The first is a feeling that the greatest danger to the incipient democracy of Spain is the faltering economy. Unless the government, by whatever means, takes swift measures to stop the economic deterioration, Spain could plummet into chaos. That could tempt the armed forces, perhaps with popular support, to step in and end the experiment with democracy after almost four decades of dictatorship.

The second is a feeling of confidence in Suárez and King Juan Carlos as leaders who sincerely want Spain to have a democratic system that differs little from those of the rest of Western Europe. Whatever its methods, the government is committed to democracy and in no way resembles the dictatorship of the late Francisco Franco. The government may be bypassing the Cortes, as the Spanish parliament is called, but the government's authority still rests on the results of the June 15 elections for the Cortes, the first freely contested elections in 41 years. These feelings are based on a good deal of political reality. Yet, to an outsider, some doubts persist. The government's need to cut democratic corners sometimes seems to come out of convenience, and not from the pressures of an emergency. Moreover, its methods tend to hide divisiveness and stifle public debate. These are so vital to the democratic process that the young Spanish democracy may be setting an unhealthy precedent in pushing them aside so soon.

The complexity of the problem is illustrated by what are

known here as the Pacts of Moncloa. The Suárez government is very proud of these pacts negotiated with the opposition. Colorful government posters are urging Spaniards to buy copies of the pacts at their news kiosks for 50 pesetas (about 60 cents). The pacts, in fact, are the envy of the government of neighboring Portugal, which is stymied by its own opposition.

The pacts came out of the Spanish government's paralysis in facing the economy. After the elections, it was obvious that something had to be done about extraordinary inflation, rising unemployment, and enormous deficits in the balance of payments. Austerity was needed. Wages had to be held down, credit cut back, public spending diminished.

Suárez had the votes to do anything he wanted. His party, the Union of the Democratic Center, had won a near majority of the seats in the Chamber of Deputies of the bicameral Cortes and a bare majority in the Senate.

But for months, Suárez did nothing. He did not want to alienate the workers and small businessmen who would feel austerity most. Moreover, a parliamentary-approved economic program might prove worthless if the labor unions opposed it with continual strikes. To placate labor, Suárez knew he also had to change the revenue system so that it covered the rich, who had been evading taxes for decades. This would alienate some of the main supporters of his own party.

The Pacts of Moncloa

Suárez did not want the onus of doing all this by himself. So he called all the political leaders of Spain to a conference at the Palace of Moncloa, his office and home, to join in working out a pact that would take Spain out of its economic crisis.

Felipe González, the leader of the Socialist party, the main opposition, was reluctant, but he had little choice. Communist leader Santiago Carrillo, whose main goal is to give his small party respectability, accepted the Suárez call immediately. If González had refused, he would have been stamped as unpatriotic.

The politicians met in secret and signed an economic pact on October 9. Its most significant provision imposed a 22 percent limit on wage increases next year, well below the current inflation rate of 30 percent. As a concession to the opposition, a political pact also was signed two weeks later in which the government accepted opposition proposals on political rights and on changes in the criminal law.

Suárez recognized that signing a pact after secret negotiations was a strange way of doing business in a parliamentary democracy. "The government understands," he said in a speech to the Cortes, "that its way of directing the political life of the country is not the usual way of governments in consolidated democratic regimes. And, at the same time, the opposition understands that it cannot always play the role assigned to it in such systems."

Suárez justified this for Spain at this time on the grounds that democracy was still weak and that the Cortes, in fact, was still writing a new, democratic constitution. Spain's present stage of political development, he said in a televised address a few days later, "is characterized by a contradiction in which we have a completely democratic situation on the surface that lacks, at the same time, a general democratic context and democratic legal rules. We are governing a country with a parliamentary system without a recent parliamentary tradition."

But the Suárez government went even further than the Pacts of Moncloa in limiting parliamentary democracy. Over the objections of the Socialist party, the government did not submit the wage-policy provision of the pacts to a vote of the Cortes. Instead, it enacted the provision by decree.

Present parliamentary rules allow this. The Cortes has a committee for urgent legislation. If the government feels there is a need for an emergency decree, it can submit the decree to the committee.

The decree is enacted if the committee agrees that an

emergency exists. Since the Suárez party controls at least seven of the 11 votes on this committee, the Suárez government can enact anything it wants by decree.

The committee meets in secret. When the wage-policy decree came before it in late November, the committee did not even debate before approving the decree with only two Socialists and a member of a minor Catalan party dissenting.

The wage-policy law would have been enacted even if the government had not issued its decree. Since all the political leaders had approved the policy in the economic Pact of Moncloa, their parties surely would have voted in favor of it in the Cortes. Then why did Suárez use the decree?

The government said that the law could not be delayed any longer. But it is hard to believe that a delay of a few days or even weeks would have mattered very much—especially since the law covers labor contracts signed even before its enactment. More important, a vote would have come only after a public debate in the Cortes—after an airing of the issues. The government of Suárez, made up mainly of bureaucrats trained under the dictatorship of the late Francisco Franco, is not comfortable with an airing of issues. It prefers agreements worked out quietly and secretly.

In an angry editorial, the newspaper *El País* attacked the penchant of the government, and the opposition as well, for working in secret.

El País said the political leaders "met in the palace of Moncloa like the executives of great multinational corporations conferring in grand hotels. Certainly they tried, as far as it was possible, to resolve the problems of the country. But they also took care to protect their corporative and professional interests as a political class, while keeping the public in ignorance . . .

"There are many dangers that lie in ambush for the democracy being born in Spain," the newspaper went on. "Not the least of which is the fact that the party leaders believe that politics can be played in the same way it was during the dictatorship and that they themselves should and can monopolize the political situation."

Spain's Critical Period

There have been other examples of Spanish politicians preferring to negotiate in secret rather than to debate in public. With the acquiescence of the opposition, the Suárez government granted provisional autonomy to the region of Catalonia by decree at the end of September. There is little doubt that a law enacting such autonomy would have passed the Cortes by an almost unanimous vote. But by enacting it through a decree, the Suárez government cut off public debate on one of the most significant decisions in Spanish history.

A few weeks ago, members of a special committee of the Cortes, charged with preparing the new constitution, became enraged when they discovered that a copy of the first draft of the constitution had been leaked to the press. The committee, comprising both members of the government party and the opposition, wanted those most involved—the Spanish people—kept in ignorance while they continued to debate and negotiate the constitutional issues.

There is little doubt that Spain is going through a critical early period of democracy. There may be a good deal of wisdom in the government's policy of avoiding controversy in tackling major issues like the state of the economy. A period of contentiousness could give the Spanish people a feeling that democracy is a weak system that accomplishes little beyond bluster. This feeling might be exaggerated if people felt that interminal argument was holding up a solution to economic problems. Spain's new democracy does need confidence.

Yet, the cultivation of confidence must be handled with care. The Spanish government has been careless, almost reckless in its willingness to stamp on democracy to save it. To gain confidence, the government of Premier Suárez is acting in an authoritarian manner, with a bureaucratic contempt for the right of the Spanish people to know what is going on. These habits, blessed in the name of democracy now, may be difficult to break later. In the long run, these attitudes may be just as dangerous to democracy as any loss of confidence.

THE SPANISH LEFT: DIVIDED BUT STRONG [6]

Spain's national elections last June, the first in 40 years, did not mark the end of fascism as heralded by the Western press. But an impressive showing by left parties in the campaign gave new impetus to the movement for democratic reform and the dismantling of the fascist apparatus. The three major parties that identify themselves as Marxist received 42 percent of the vote; the Socialist PSOE 29 percent, the Communist party (PCE) nine percent, and the independent Popular Socialist party four percent. Premier Adolfo Suárez's Union of the Democratic Center—the coalition of ex-loyalists, much loved by the American government, who supported the Franco regime but now vaguely advocate reform—had hoped for an absolute majority but polled only 34 percent. And the Francoist Popular Alliance, considered a formidable obstacle at the beginning of the campaign, got only eight percent.

The election "reform" enacted by the Suárez government, however, virtually guaranteed that the center would remain in control of the Spanish Cortes (the bicameral parliament). Both government campaign financing and parliament seats were apportioned according to a gerrymandered system that gives extra weight to large parties and rural areas while penalizing smaller parties and urban districts. With only a third of the popular vote, the center party got a near majority (47 percent) of the senate seats. The Socialists won in every city except Madrid, where they ran only two percentage points behind Suárez. Moreover, the constitution inherited from Franco gives the King power to

[6] From "The Spanish Left: Divided But Surprisingly Strong," by Temma Kaplan and Jon Wiener. Ms. Kaplan is an associate professor of history at the University of California, Los Angeles, and author of *Anarchists of Andalusia*. Mr. Wiener is an associate professor of history at the University of California at Irvine. *Working Papers for a New Society*. 6:20-4. Ja./F. '78. Copyright 1978 by the Center for the Study of Public Policy, Inc. Reprinted with permission.

appoint 41 of the 245 senators. These appointments, not surprisingly, all went to Francoists and center party moderates.

The Need for Constitutional Reform

The first order of business for the left in Spain is constitutional reform. Simply to make Spain a liberal democracy will require extensive changes that the center, disappointed by the June elections, has little incentive to make. Basic civil liberties and freely elected municipal and regional governments are the prerequisites for a strong Socialist movement in Spain. Implementing these reforms will require sustained popular pressure mobilized by the progressive parties.

The Franco constitution does not guarantee freedom of speech or association. The King retains the right to rule by decree. He declared trade unions legal last spring but could abolish them at any time by a similar order. The *guardia civil* continues to enforce frequent bans on political meetings, rallies, and demonstrations. Last summer's campaign began with police rampages throughout the Basque provinces in which five people were killed. Many of the far left parties were not legalized until a month after the voting, and even then police broke up their public celebration in Madrid on the ground that they did not have a permit to demonstrate.

The fascist state apparatus remains intact. The government, supported by the army, is responsible to the King rather than to the elected Cortes, which may advise the King but cannot make law. Every government official, from the small town mayors to the premier himself, is a holdover from the old regime. The Cortes is drafting a new constitution that will determine how soon municipal and provincial elections are held—elections in which the left is expected to defeat the center in most cities and in several of the provinces of Catalonia and Andalusia. The left wants the new Cortes to disband once the constitutional issues are resolved, cutting short Suárez's term and calling for new national

elections that the Socialists might even win. Center domina-
tion of the Cortes, however, makes this unlikely.

Spain is also facing an economic crisis. The country now
has over a million unemployed and an inflation rate of 30
percent. Business, fearing a strengthened trade union movement and left gains in future elections, is not investing in
new plants and equipment. The multinational corporations
are recommending strict wage controls and an austerity
program that would lower the standard of living and, they
say, encourage investment. In July Suárez was forced to de-
value the peseta by 20 percent.

Socialists and Communists alike are grateful that it is
Suárez who will have to put an austerity program into effect,
leaving them to act as the opposition without having to
come up with a program of their own. At present the left's
economic strategy is essentially defensive. They oppose wage
controls and support full rights for trade unions, which,
despite their much-heralded legalization last year, still are
not allowed to operate inside factories or negotiate contracts.
The Communists have called for a "just wage," higher pensions for the elderly and disabled, taxes on corporate and
individual income, and protection for small businesses
against monopolies. But neither the Communists nor the
Socialists have put forward a positive economic alternative.

Differences Among the Spanish Left

Beyond the most basic issues of political and economic
reform, there are real differences among the major parties of
the Spanish left. The Socialists' strong showing at the polls
last summer can be attributed at least partially to their
adoption of left positions cautiously avoided by the Communist party: support for the militant Basque nationalists,
opposition to US military bases in Spain and to Spain's
involvement in the Common Market, open criticism of
Suárez's policies and of his origins in the old Franco establishment. These issues are by no means the center of the
Socialists' program, but they are points of genuine difference
from the Communists.

The Spanish Communist party's long history as the only continuous organized left resistance to Franco has been both an asset and a liability in an open political arena. Forty years of propaganda against the underground PCE succeeded in convincing many people that the Communists were responsible for every plane hijacking, every terrorist attack, every political killing. When door-to-door canvassers in Barcelona told one housewife in a lower-middle-class neighborhood that they were Communists, she turned pale and whispered, "Have you come to kidnap me?" and then fainted. But since Franco branded every act of opposition to his regime as Communist-inspired, many antifascists have traditionally supported the party as the only means by which they could struggle against fascism.

Others on the left still hold the PCE accountable for its role in the Civil War of 1936–1939. Dominated by Stalinists and eager to win middle-class support, the party forcibly dismantled workers and peasants collectives and jailed and assassinated anti-Stalinists and anarchists. The advanced age of most PCE leaders—in a country where two-thirds of the population is under 40, the premier 43, and the head of the socialists 35—reinforces the impression that the PCE represents the Civil War old guard. The party today, however, does not defend its actions during the Civil War, preferring to focus on its leadership of the post-Civil War resistance.

There is also a pervasive fear, not altogether unfounded, that Communist successes will provoke a military coup. Last winter Premier Suárez promised the heads of the armed forces that he would never legalize the PCE. In the early spring he said that he would consider legalizing it only after the election. But the real possibility that none of the left parties would participate in the elections if the PCE were excluded convinced Suárez to grant legal recognition to the party in April. Scarcely a month later the Communists, after 40 years of brutal repression, turned out 200,000 supporters for a rally in Barcelona, mustered a similar number in Madrid, and held smaller rallies around the country. The demonstrators knew party chants and songs and the political histories of PCE leaders, many of whom had spent half their lives in jail or exile. The army chiefs were said to be enraged, but they took no action.

The PCE is pursuing a policy of relentless moderation, arguing that socialism is a long way off and that fascism will be abolished, not by armed struggle of workers and peasants, but rather by a series of peaceful, democratic reforms supported by substantial sections of the "national bourgeoisie" and the lower middle class. The PCE has abandoned the dictatorship of the proletariat as a goal and has been sharply critical of the Soviet model of socialism. Party secretary Santiago Carrillo is in fact one of the leading theoreticians of Eurocommunist gradualism, and as such has been singled out for attack by the Soviet leadership.

Since the elections the PCE has been a loyal supporter of the Suárez government and of King Juan Carlos. Lacking a majority in parliament, the government must find allies in order to pass its programs. While the Socialists have maintained the critical stance of an opposition party, giving Suárez only selective support, the Communists have backed every major government proposal, including wage and price controls. A nationwide strike wave last fall thus challenged not only the Suárez government but the PCE as well.

As a reward for PCE moderation, Santiago Carrillo became the first European Communist leader to visit the United States. He returned the compliment by keeping his lecture appointment at Yale even though it meant crossing the picket line of striking university workers after negotiations for an off-campus lecture site broke down in confusion. He began his talk by denouncing America's trade union leadership as corrupt and unworthy of support.

It remains to be seen whether the PCE—which campaigned on such slogans as "To vote Communist is to vote for democracy" and "Liberty and more liberty"—can demonstrate a genuine commitment to democracy within its own party. Forty years as an underground organization dependent on Moscow for its very existence did not foster a tradition of internal democracy. The first public party congress, tentatively scheduled for February 1978, should make it clear whether the PCE will permit serious debate over party policy and structure.

The largest left party, the Socialist PSOE, is not considered by the old Franco establishment to pose a serious threat, despite its more radical position on some issues. The generals raised no objection to the legalization of the PSOE, and its new leadership has never been locked inside Franco's prisons. Founded in 1879 as the Marxist party in Spain, the PSOE was the largest political organization in the country before the Civil War. But it was not able to maintain more than a shadow presence in Spain after 1939; its leadership went into exile and grew old.

The new PSOE is synonymous with its leader, the handsome young labor lawyer Felipe Gonzáles. Casual and charismatic, "Felipe," as he is universally known, organized a group of independent Socialists in Seville during the early 1970s. In 1973 they confronted the old PSOE leadership in exile and audaciously took over the party.

The PSOE has two distinct wings, which may increasingly come into conflict. The more conservative leadership draws both financial and ideological support from the German social democratic party of Willy Brandt (PSOE campaign posters featured blond children and Alpine landscapes). The party's left wing is rooted in the trade union movement, sings the "Internationale," and flies the red flag. The Socialists have won over many workers with the argument that PSOE has a real chance of bringing a Socialist government to Spain in the next few years. In the weeks following the elections, 7,000 workers joined the Socialist UGT union.

Some observers outside the party predict that the right wing, with its German backing, will drive the left out of the PSOE and into the Communist party. Numerically that would be a small proportion of the Socialists' vote, but it would mark the loss of some of their best-organized and most authentically working-class sections. Compared to the militant and well-organized base of the PCE, PSOE supporters are relatively passive. A cab driver in Seville the day before the summer elections denounced Felipe as a "liar, like all politicians," but admitted that he planned to vote for him. "Politics is like a lottery," he explained. "The odds are against you, but you never know when you might win."

The Regional Autonomy Issue

The issue of regional autonomy will undoubtedly play a large part in the future of the Spanish left, as it did in the June elections. The Communists refused to support the Basques' "week of struggle for amnesty" last May—a militant public demonstration that bordered on mass insurrection in the Basque industrial cities. Instead the PCE denounced political violence in any form, and even sent telegrams of condolence to the widows of policemen killed by leftists during the campaign. This position certainly cost the Communists votes, not only in the Basque provinces, but also in such PCE strongholds as the working-class sections of Madrid, where police have frequently battled with leftists.

Demands for regional autonomy in a less militant context, however, have been a source of strength for the Communists. Spain is the only country in the world where the Communist Third International recognized two official Communist parties: the Spanish PCE and the United Socialist parties of Catalonia (PSUC). The bustling port city of Barcelona is the center of what seems like a separate country. Catalonia has drawn workers by the thousands from poorer parts of Spain to its booming factories and its century-old tradition of trade union militance. The Catalan bourgeoisie, large and prosperous, prides itself on its cosmopolitan culture, its liberal politics, and its undying hostility to Franco and his legacy of repression.

In the wake of the Civil War, Franco took away the right to self-government Catalonia had been granted by the Republic in 1932. He made it a crime to speak Catalan (a language distinct from Spanish, halfway to French), to display the Catalan flag, or to dance the *sardana*, a regional circle dance. In a region that has traditionally had its own political parties as well as its own culture, the left and liberals agree that autonomy is the number one political priority. They demand a regional government that has powers of taxation and control of the schools and police—essentially the powers of an American state. A long anti-Franco tradition has made the left in Catalonia much stronger than in the nation as a whole. PSUG, which claims the allegiance of many of Catalonia's leading artists and intellectuals, is so much stronger than the PCE that some say "the PCE is PSUC's branch in Spain."

Last summer's elections proved Barcelona to be one of the great "red cities" of Europe. Communists and Socialists together got exactly 50 percent of the vote. The Communist ran five percentage points ahead of the center party, polling a surprising 20 percent. Genuine autonomy for Catalonia would almost certainly mean a government of Socialists and Communists, one that could offer a concrete alternative to the centrist powers in Madrid.

The Feminist Movement and the Left

Spain's left parties must still come to terms with the country's growing feminist movement. The feminists have defined three key issues. First is the abolition of an 1889 law that makes adultery a criminal offense and defines it in such a way that husbands cannot be found guilty. Second is the legalization of divorce, for which there is widespread support. Third and most important is the legalization of abortion and the free distribution of contraceptives—volatile issues in Catholic Spain.

Both the Socialists and the Communists have officially endorsed all three demands, but they have not given them a high priority. Communist party secretary Santiago Carrillo infuriated many of his female supporters by ignoring them throughout last summer's campaign and then making a dramatic plea for legal abortion two nights before the elections.

Feminists fear that both the Socialists and the Communists would be willing to compromise their stand on abortion in return for Catholic votes. In both parties women have little to say about party tactics in pursuit of feminist objectives and are grossly underrepresented in leadership positions. Except for the 80-year-old Dolores Ibarurri, "La Passionara," who herself has no interest in feminism, there are few women on the PCE central committee and only one among the elected deputies from Barcelona. At Communist rallies the male rank-and-file actively ignores women speakers.

The leading feminist group in Catalonia split in the late spring, largely over how and whether to participate in the elections. The largest splinter joined with a moderate liberal group, forming one of those odd electoral coalitions to which European feminists are increasingly drawn for lack of serious consideration by major parties on the left. Only Maoist electoral coalitions such as the "Workers' Candidacies" made a special effort to attract women and give them real power. Their campaigns stressed equal rights, child care, and abortion. In parts of the South, where the electorate is reputed to be the most chauvinist, their slates were almost exclusively women.

Anarchists, Trotskyists, and Others

There are many small groups of anarchists, Trotskyists, and Maoists active in Spain. About 20 of these groups asked for but were denied legal recognition before last summer's elections. Some ad hoc coalitions like the "Workers' Candidacies" and the Trotskyist "Front for Workers Unity" were allowed to run slates but attracted only a negligible vote. In general, the far left groups reject electoral politics and warn of fostering "parliamentary illusions."

Spain had the largest anarchist movement in history during the first part of the twentieth century, with nearly one million members in its union, the National Confederation of Labor (CNT). After the Civil War, the anarchists tried to maintain a militant underground organization in Spain. But lacking the kind of institutional support that the Soviet Union provided to the PCE, they were unsuccessful.

The Communists went on to gain control of the underground trade union movement, and today the Communist-dominated Workers' Commission claims 175,000 members while the CNT has no more than 30,000. The CNT allows only workers to be members, however, and this figure does not reflect the CNT's significant base of support among students, particularly at the universities in Barcelona and Madrid. The students and some faculty consider themselves *acratas*, a term roughly meaning libertarian and *gauchiste*. The *acratas* have been active in university struggles such as the year-long fight to win job security for teaching assistants and nonacademic employees like secretaries and porters. They reject electoral politics and did not participate in last summer's elections.

The CNT expressed its opposition to the PCE's strategy of electoral gradualism by organizing a "libertarian festival" in mid-July, one month after the election. Half a million young people came from all over Europe to make Barcelona the "world capital of libertarianism" for three days. Sexual liberation and ecology were the leading themes; "libertinism is liberty" the slogan. Where the CNT of the thirties organized its massive working-class base into militant trade unions, the new anarchist youth mix antiauthoritarianism and anti-Marxism with rock music, feminism, gay liberation, nudism, and dope.

The Trotskyists and the Maoists continue to attack the PCE's Eurocommunist politics as reformist. This charge is not without its supporters. When the PCE announced that it no longer sought the dictatorship of the proletariat, one Communist worker grumbled, "Now they've given away *our* dictatorship." In opposition to the PCE's strategy of class alliances, the Trotskyists call for a single working-class organization that would oppose the entire bourgeoisie and campaign directly for a Socialist state. Although the real battle in the electoral arena will be between the Communists and the Socialists, the far left groups have established a presence in the trade union movement; the Trotskyists have won members in the Basque country and the Maoists have some strength in Barcelona. Nearly all of the far left has disowned the terrorist groups GRAPO and ETA-IV, suggesting that if they are not fascist creations, they "objectively" serve the far right.

Spain's political situation is rich with possibilities for the left. The fascists have discovered that their base of support is tiny. The ruling center party, with less popular support than it thought it had, will have to take unpopular economic measures that in the short run can only strengthen the left. The Socialist PSOE is likely to win power in the big cities as soon as municipal elections are held and national power in the foreseeable future. But as the PCE has accurately perceived, the process of demolishing the fascist state is still in its early stages and may yet encounter strong resistance. The left may be up from underground, but it is not yet out of the fascist woods.

SPAIN'S SOCIALISTS JUST LEFT OF CENTER [7]

Spain's two main political bodies are maneuvering into position for the expected battle between right and left next year. On April 30th, the small Popular Socialist party merged its forces into the much bigger Socialist Workers' party, led by the youthful Mr. Felipe González, in preparation for the coming challenge to Mr. Adolfo Suárez's right-of-center government.

Until recently, Spain's democratic right and left had been the best of allies, helping each other to find a way out of the authoritarian wilderness of the Franco era and to avoid giving Spain's right-wing army any excuse to lead them back there. Their tacit cooperation was extended last October, when the governing Union of the Democratic Center signed the Moncloa Pact with the left-wing parties to control the bucking economy and to draw up a new democratic constitution. The result was that for a time formal opposition almost vanished. The Socialist Workers occasion-

    [7] From "A Schmidt, Not a Mitterrand?" The Economist. 267:16. My. 6, '78.
© The Economist Newspaper Ltd., London, 1978. Reprinted with permission.

ally waxed indignant about excesses committed by Francoists still lurking in the armed forces, the police and the
prison services. But otherwise they left Mr. Suárez gener-
ously alone. The constitution was hammered out in committee behind closed doors. The Socialist Workers and the
Communists made their trade union friends respect a gov-
ernment-set wage ceiling. In return Mr. Suárez, who two
years ago was the minister running the single party in a
one-party state, made himself look almost like a social democrat.

But Mr. Suárez began to move rightwards again in
March, when he fired the ministers responsible for the economic provisions of the Moncloa Pact, headed by the left-
of-center Mr. Fuentes Quintana. Mr. Fuentes's plans for
raising taxes and enlarging state control had been raising the
hackles of conservative members of the Democratic Center.
Economic ministers more sympathetic to business were appointed. Mr. Suárez also seems to be preparing against
Socialist and Communist opposition, to apply to join
NATO.

The government is increasingly trying to steamroller the
committee drafting the constitution. In March, the Socialist
Workers' representative on the committee walked out in
protest against government proposals to give employers the
constitutional right of lockout and to maintain the protected status of the Roman Catholic church. Mr. Suárez is
diluting the powers to be given to Spain's regions by insist-
ing that Madrid retain a veto over their decisions and tax
systems. He has also made a major show of his authority by
delaying Spain's first free local elections, which the left
wanted to be held at the end of last year, until the new constitution is approved by referendum—which could push
them into next year.

Mr. Suárez's party has just enough seats in Parliament
to govern without the consent of the left-wing parties if it
gets the support of the small right-wing Popular Alliance.
But the Prime Minister has so far got away with needling
his Socialist partners without their walking out of the

Moncloa Pact. This is because they do not want national power in 1978. Spain's inflation—at 26 percent last year easily the worst among the big economies of western Europe —is slowly being brought down. But the cost has been a sharp drop in the living standards of most people and an industrial recession, both of which are chipping remorselessly away at Mr. Suárez's popularity. This year inflation could drop into the teens. The Socialist Workers would prefer to wait for power at least until next year, when the economy would be easier to handle.

Moderation Pays Again

As things now stand, the left has an excellent chance of winning the next election. Opinion poll leads can melt away on polling day, as France's election proved in March. But at the last Spanish election in June the two Socialist parties between them level-pegged the Democratic Center in numbers of votes, though not in seats. Since then, the left has led the government in the opinion polls by an ever-widening margin.

Mr. Felipe González's Socialists have improved their prospects by showing themselves to be anything but the loony left many people feared in Spain after Franco's death. The party's history has not always been one of moderation. But it was bankrolled by West Germany's Social Democrats when it was reduced to a semiclandestine opposition before 1976. When it came back into the open as a mass party last year some Spaniards expected the party's radicals, led by its deputy leader, Mr. Alfonso Guerra, to reassert themselves. But Mr. González has managed to hold his party's major proposals for reform down to (long overdue) tax reforms and to the nationalization of the sort of industries already state-controlled in most European countries.

The Socialist Workers, if they come to power, may have trouble satisfying the expectations they have aroused. Their manifesto last June was lavish in promises of a welfare state, which Spain is unlikely to be able to afford unless the economy improves sharply. But Spain's Socialists have one advantage over Britain's, in that the unions' influence on them is relatively small. And they have another over the French Socialists—that they do not have to worry about being too moderate for fear of losing support to an aggressively working-class Communist party. The policies of Mr. Carrillo's Spanish Communists are if anything more cautious than those of the Socialists. The moderation of the Socialist Workers, if it lasts, augurs well for an enduring two-party system in Spain.

II. SPAIN'S ECONOMY

EDITOR'S INTRODUCTION

Section II is concerned with the Spanish economic picture. Dr. Joaquin Muns, professor of economics, University of Barcelona, comments on the steps taken to restore Spain's economy to health. A contributor to the magazine *Swiss Review of World Affairs*, Walter Günthardt notes an alarming drift towards inflation and unemployment and an imbalance of payments. The last two articles in the section by James M. Markham, a special correspondent for the New York *Times*, examine the political repercussions of Spain's economic crisis and the looming income tax reforms and devaluations that are likely to evolve for Spaniards generally.

RESTORING SPAIN'S ECONOMY [1]

The elections of June 1977 marked a watershed for the Spanish economy no less than for its political system. Politically, they constituted the first occasion for 40 years in which the real relative strengths of all the Spanish political parties and ideologies could be tested within a democratic constitutional framework. The outcome showed that two years of skillful maneuvering by King Juan Carlos and the political tact of President Suárez had proved decisive in preparing the country to enter the age of democracy with a degree of smoothness which was surprising by any standards. Economically, the elections marked the point at which the long-

[1] From "Spain: the New Wind of Realism," by Joaquin Muns, professor of economics, University of Barcelona, Spain. *The Banker*. 128:57-65. Ap. '78. © The Financial Times Limited 1978. Reprinted from The Banker with the Editor's permission.

delayed adjustment of the Spanish economy to the effects of the oil price increase could no longer be put off.

The results of these elections are well known. The victory of Sr Suárez's centrist alliance and the strength shown by the Socialist opposition were probably one of the best combinations the country could have been granted to bring the transitional period to a successful conclusion without unexpected shocks. President Suárez realized full well that his triumph at the polls was no blank check, but rather the acknowledgement of his skill in steering the country clear of some of the worst dangers that had been feared. The Socialist vote and the relative failure of the rightist Alianza Popular, headed by Sr Fraga Iribarne, must have brought Sr Suárez the message that what the country really wanted were decisive policies and changes to be implemented peacefully.

Where this message bore particular meaning and urgency was in the economic field. Spain had not been spared by the international oil crisis, but none of the governments which had ruled the country since 1973, including General Franco's last ministries, had made any real effort to overcome the effects of the crisis. The old dictator was too weak to act promptly and courageously; King Juan Carlos and his first governments, in the face of a very complex and delicate situation, made the deliberate choice of buying time for the transitional period, at whatever price. This led, however, to the unnecessary and almost suicidal conclusion that the delay in the adjustment process to the new international economic conditions had to be considered part of that unavoidable price.

The neglect of the economic problem had made it almost intractable by the eve of the June elections. Inflation, at an annual rate, was approaching 30 percent, and the current account deficit in the first half of 1977 pointed an almost unsustainable $5 billions mark for the whole year, as against an already excessive $4.3 billions figure in 1976. Neither the modest GDP growth rate of 3–3½ percent nor the unemployment rate of 5.1 percent which the economy recorded by mid-1977 could be considered satisfactory. No wonder the general impression among economists in the middle of last year was that the country was in a real *impasse*.

The Moncloa Agreements

It was quite clear that if the elections were to mean anything President Suárez had to grasp a fistful of nettles, the biggest of which was the economic one. For this, he needed not only to restrain his instinct to shy away from the subject of economics—where he feels uneasy—but also find a good and trustworthy economist to nurse the economy back to health. Realism again came to his aid; the appointment of Professor E. Fuentes Quintana as economic superminister with the rank of second vice-president of the government (the first vice-president being the defense minister) was no doubt one of the best—if not the best—choices possible at that moment, since he is a widely respected economist with a moderate and progressive approach to social and economic problems. This was what the country needed.

The government's new team of economists immediately took the unavoidable and long overdue measure of devaluing the peseta, to which I shall refer later, and then decided to shut themselves away until they had drafted a complete recovery plan for the Spanish economy. Apprehensive of the social unrest which might be triggered off by the program, President Suárez decided to summon all the parties and political alliances represented in Parliament and negotiate with them the acceptance of a package deal incorporating both the economic program prepared by Professor Fuentes's team and a bundle of political measures aimed at updating some crucial pieces of legislation. The strategy worked out as planned and the so-called Moncloa Agreements were signed by all the parties in October 25 1977, and ratified by Parliament soon after. (The Moncloa Agreements take their name from the Moncloa Palace, the official residence of the Spanish President of the government, where the talks between Sr Suárez and the political parties took place.)

Restoring the Economy to Health

The economic package, which makes up the bulk of the Agreements, has two very distinct parts. The first consists of an array of measures intended to have a strong short-run impact, so as to make the economy accomplish its long-delayed adjustment and, after having recovered its health, grow again at a reasonable speed. These measures can be grouped under the following five headings:

(a) A higher degree of self-control on the part of the *public sector*. To this end, the program set limits to public current expenditures (+21.4 percent in 1978), to the 1978 overall government budgetary deficit (ptas 73 billions) and to the increase in the 1978 social security contributions of both employers and employees (+18 percent). At the same time, the government agreed to increase its investment expenditures by 30 percent in 1978 while stepping up its share of the social security bill to 8.2 percent, as against only 3.5 percent in 1977.

(b) In the field of *monetary policy*, the Agreements embodied a commitment by the government to scale down gradually the rate of growth of money supply from the 20-21 percent rate at which it was growing by mid-1977 to an average of 17 percent for the whole year 1978. Other measures agreed upon set limits to existing privileged channels of credit, while trying to make this and other types of credit more easily available to small- and medium-size firms.

(c) As far as *prices* are concerned, the Moncloa Agreements did not go beyond a pledge to control all those which can bear heavily on the cost of living or belong to sectors which operate under monopolistic conditions.

(d) In the potentially explosive area of *incomes policy*, the document set an upper limit of 22 percent for the rate of growth in 1978 of the total amount of wages and salaries. Firms which are forced to accept higher claims will be allowed to sack five percent of their labor force. Except for this case, no mention was made of softening the old Franco laws which made lay-offs impossible, except under conditions of severe hardship for the firm.

(e) Finally, the government committed itself to follow a more aggressive *job-creating policy*, while at the same time raising the unemployment compensations to more realistic levels.

All these measures were expected to have a relatively rapid impact on the economy. As a matter of fact, the program aimed at reducing the rate of inflation from the 1977 average rate to an average rate of 22 percent in 1978 and 12 percent in 1979 (or 15 and 10 percent on a December-to-December basis). As for the foreign sector, the targets were a maximum current account deficit of $2.8 billions in 1978 and $1.9 billions in 1979. Finally, the unemployment rate was expected to be adversely affected by the deflationary effect of all the measures implemented, but only in 1978.

The second part of the economic package of the Moncloa Agreements contained a long list of declarations about policies affecting social and economic activities and sectors as well as the framework of the economic system itself. It is impossible to go into details of all these objectives, but it can be stated in very general terms that they combine and introduce a mixture with varying degrees of rationalization, democratic control and even some mild socialistic tendencies. This part of the economic package as well as the political chapter of the Moncloa Agreements are to be interpreted as part of the price the opposition charged for endorsing a document which made no effort to conceal its character as a typically market-economy-oriented solution for the short run.

Making Up the Lost Time

As the Moncloa Agreements had been agreed upon and signed by all the main political parties, the main question was whether the trade unions and the employers' associations would endorse them. Although in somewhat ambiguous terms, the former were fairly quick to do so—no big surprise given the connections between the two main trade unions (the Socialist UGT and the Communist Comisiones Obreras), and the Socialist (PSOE) and Communist (PCE) parties. The employers' reaction was at first openly hostile. They accused the government of carrying out a leftist policy and also blamed the Agreements for keeping intact the Francoist legislation concerning the dismissal of redundant workers.

These and other objections have been gradually smoothed away. Two factors have played a crucial role here: on the one hand, the government has made clear that this time it means business, and that the Agreements would be respected to the last letter; on the other hand, the performance of the Spanish economy has improved markedly since last summer.

It is fair to say that at least up to the time of this writing (March) the Moncloa Agreements are being complied with. In general, the wage and salaries limits are being respected, and this part of the program was of course the most problematic one. The public sector is making an effort to put its house in order and the dynamic and skillful Minister of Finance, Sr Fernández Ordóñez, has lost no time in laying the foundations of the fiscal reform the country has been waiting for so long. Obviously the deep-rooted Spanish habit of evading taxes cannot easily be altered; but the introduction of new penalties and the revision of the bank secrecy laws as applied to fiscal purposes reveal a more resolute political will to modernize the Spanish fiscal system.

In some cases, compliance with the Moncloa Agreements has even gone beyond the agreed targets. Such is the case of monetary policy, where the growth rates of the money supply dropped quickly during the last quarter of 1977. Given the state of the Spanish economy, the considerable delay with which the country is facing the adjustment process, and the rather slow pace of this adjustment embodied in the Agreements, this monetary tightness, which is in the process of being corrected, can be considered a blessing in disguise.

The Spanish economy seems to be reacting as expected

to the treatment administered to it. The rate of growth of GDP slowed down considerably during the second half of 1977 and the opening months of this year, probably falling to zero. This is a considerable downturn from the 3–3½ percent at which it was growing by mid-1977 and it echoes the type of serious adjustment other countries undertook as early as 1974 or 1975. Experts do not expect any appreciable upswing until the second half of this year, or at least this is what they say should happen if the present gains are not to be wasted.

Successes So Far

The government has made its priorities quite clear: they are to slow down inflation, close the external deficit, and reduce unemployment—in that order. So far, results have accorded well with this ranking. As far as inflation is concerned, the rate of increase of consumer prices has dropped down from a monthly average of 2.6 percent during the first nine months of 1977 to a monthly rate of 1.2 percent for the four months up to January 1978. Even more important, one can detect a noticeable reduction in the psychological element of the inflationary syndrome.

The success on the inflationary front has been exceeded by the performance of the external sector of the Spanish economy since last summer. While the current account deficit of the first semester of 1977 had reached the daunting figure of $2.3 billions, the corresponding amount for the second half of that year decreased dramatically to a mere $0.4 billion. This sudden change was of such a magnitude that at the end of 1977 Spanish foreign reserves (at $6.1 billions) had regained the mid-1974 level.

This turn of events in the foreign sector of the Spanish economy is not of course a miracle and several important factors may help to explain it. First and possibly foremost, the new government took, as early as July, the necessary step of devaluing the peseta, by as much as 20 percent; this brought the rate of exchange of the peseta to a realistic level for the first time since 1971. Second, domestic demand has been at long last handled with the necessary degree of firmness. Finally, the gradual progress that has been made in defining both the economic and political terms of reference within which the country is to work has brought an added measure of certainty much welcomed by Spaniards and foreigners alike.

There is little doubt that this improvement of the foreign sector of the Spanish economy is real, but one should not forget the high cost—economic standstill. Special factors, such as leads and lags, have undoubtedly played a part, and the extent of the underlying improvement is not clear. The implication of this is, however, plain: the Spanish authorities will need to await a further improvement of the foreign accounts before they unleash the economy. Meanwhile the present level of the Spanish foreign debt, estimated at $13.1 billions (of which probably half is public) and the newly-comfortable level of foreign reserves should make the foreign sector one of the least troublesome in the next months, provided that a realistic rate of exchange policy is strictly adhered to (which, given the tradition of the country, is unfortunately by no means sure).

Unemployment—the Necessary Price

Miracles do not exist in economies and the rate of unemployment has obviously reflected the hardships imposed on the economy. According to the latest available figures, the number of unemployed had reached 831,000, or 6.3 percent of the labor force, at the end of 1977. This total is 152,000 higher than the mid-year figure, or an increase of 25 percent of the number of unemployed in six months. That Spanish society has hitherto accepted this as a necessary price for the correction of past mistakes and omissions does not mean that the country is unaware of the potentially dangerous character of the problem.

It is too early to tell whether the unexpected and sudden resignation of Professor Fuentes Quintana will lead to far-reaching changes. This led to a reshuffle of President Suárez's government in March affecting mainly the economic ministries. Sr Fernando Abril Martorell, a close friend of the President and (unlike Sr Fuentes) a member of his Unión de Centro Democrático party, took over the Vice-presidency of Economic Affairs, although it seems that some of the responsibilities Sr Fuentes took in his hands may go back to the Ministry of Finance. The government has made known emphatically that the Moncloa Agreements will continue to be adhered to in spite of the changes.

True, there is no doubt that "rightist" elements are trying to force some changes in the Moncloa Agreements which make them more palatable to the private sector. On the other hand, important elements of Professor Fuentes Quintana's team have taken over key positions: Sr José Ramón Alvárez Rendueles as Governor of the Bank of Spain; Sr J. L. Leal as Secretary of State for Economic Affairs; and Señores Fuentes Quintana himself and Lagares as Advisers to the President. Nobody knows whether this means that their influence will continue undiminished or if it is simply the first stage of a deeper change of tack. What is clear to the present author is that any sudden veering of the economic policy followed by the government could be extremely harmful.

On the present evidence, one can conclude that the Spanish economy has, after three and a half years of unnecessary delay, taken the orthodox and painful road leading to the unavoidable adjustment made necessary by the international oil crisis. So far, the economy has reacted with unexpected resilience to the remedies applied and the improvements are tangible. The real danger lies ahead; it is that a premature feeling of victory or simply a collective loss of patience may stunt the still young and feeble recovery.

ALARM IN THE SPANISH ECONOMY [2]

The pulsating life of the Spanish capital at present shows symptoms which are relatively new for Spain. Though un-

[2] Article by Walter Günthardt, contributor. *Swiss Review of World Affairs.* 27:8-10. N. '77. Reprinted by permission.

mistakably Iberian (that is, to some extent comparable to the situation in Portugal), they are also reminiscent of earlier phases in the economic development of Italy. This is especially true of the attitude of large segments of the population, which are ignoring—or shrugging off as exaggerated—the loudly repeated warnings from industrial and banking circles and pessimistic comments from the press. But it also applies to the attitude of the government, which thus far in the realm of economic policy has confined itself to mere verbal promises without further consequences.

There are, however, some quite specific reasons for this economic policy vacuum, linked primarily to Spain's transition to democracy. During the gradual release of the country from Franco's political legacy, Premier Adolfo Suárez and his cabinet were obviously much concerned to avoid any widely unpopular economic measures in order not to place any additional burdens on the already difficult process of democratization. Up until the June 15 elections the government largely succeeded in that aim, to an extent that was widely applauded both at home and abroad.

But now, critical voices (and by no means only those from the extreme ends of the political spectrum) are decrying that stance as an "election gift" which could turn out to be a serious danger to the consolidation of democracy in Spain. According to one well-founded argument, in order to be effective at all, the means available to correct a negative development in a given economy must be applied all the more forcefully the longer a government waits to do something about the situation. And since all the relevant economic indicators now leave no doubt that the Madrid government has remained economically passive for far too long, the interventionary measures which have become urgently needed may prove even more unpopular—and thus politically more upsetting—than they would have if they had been applied in time.

One indication of the ignorance prevalent in broad segments of the Spanish population about the country's deteriorating economic position may be seen in the surprise with which the public greeted the 25 percent devaluation of the peseta undertaken last July 12. But that surprised reaction must be seen against the background of the fact that the Vice Premier for Economic Affairs, Professor Fuentes Quintana, waited until four days prior to the devaluation before making a nationwide TV appearance in which he used hard figures to clearly underscore the gravity of the situation. And yet, on the basis of available statistics, for some time there had been no shortage of acute alarm signals indicating the steady and accelerating negative developments in most sectors of the national economy. As early as the beginning of this year, for example, the economic report of a major Spanish bank summed up the anticipated trends for 1977 as follows: "The entire country is living beyond its means; companies are holding back on investments and the politicians are leaving the urgent tasks to their successors."

In other words, most economic experts regarded an eventual devaluation of the peseta as inevitable. They were surprised only by the choice of a time, since foreign currency earnings from tourism, which reach a climax in the third quarter of each year, constitute one of the most important positive items in Spain's overall earnings picture. In point of fact, however, the devaluation was a long-overdue emergency measure which the government could no longer delay once the elections were over. This is clearly shown by the fact that support of the peseta at its old foreign-exchange level had cost the country no less than one billion dollars in hard currency during the first half of 1977, due largely to a massive flight of capital. Despite this, the devaluation offers no solution to the problems presently facing the Spanish economy, especially since the flanking measures which were initially proposed have thus far not been carried out.

Three Negative Developments

The serious consequences of the Suárez government's inactivity in the realm of economic policy are expressed largely in three negative developments, which admittedly began back in 1974 but have since been accentuated. The first and most important problem-complex is the country's balance on current account (i.e., trade balance plus balance of services and monetary transfers), which showed rising surpluses from 1969 to 1973 (reaching a maximum of $500 million) but since then has experienced an increasingly deficit trend. The 1974 deficit was $3.24 billion, in 1975 $3.54 billion, 1976 $4.25 billion, and the most pessimistic estimates for 1977 are around $5 billion.

Important in this context is the observation that the growing deficit in the balance on current account is largely due to the trend of the trade balance. For structural reasons the trade balance has consistently showed deficits in recent decades, but until 1973 those gaps had been increasingly covered by the growing surplus from the service sector. But, while there was little important change up to 1976 in the two leading items of the service balance—income from tourism, and monetary transfers from Spaniards working abroad —the nation's trade balance deficit doubled from $3.54 billion in 1973 to $7.05 billion in 1974. Since then, the increase in the value of imports has been consistently greater than that of exports, with the result that the drop in net earnings from tourism, which slipped from $2.7 billion in 1975 to $1.88 billion in 1976, placed an additional burden on the balance of current account.

At the same time, a glance at the main positions on the trade balance shows that its fundamental imbalance is largely due to oil imports. While the total value of Spain's imports rose from $8.93 billion to $16.27 billion between 1973 and 1976, expenditures for imports of liquid fuels in the same period rose from $1.28 billion to no less than $5.02 billion. During those same years the total value of Spanish exports increased from $5.39 billion to only $8.99 billion. This means that, unlike many other European countries, Spain has not yet found (or seriously searched for) a way to compensate for the oil price hike of 1973–4, either through greater efforts at increasing its exports or through cutting back its energy consumption. On the contrary: With steeply rising nominal wages, and decreasing productivity, Spain's export dynamism has taken a tangible drop. At the same time its hunger for imports continues to increase, especially for energy-gobbling household appliances and, with increasing motorization of the country, for expensive automobiles.

Galloping Inflation and Unemployment

The most blatant result of this combination of unfavorable factors is Spain's second major economic problem: galloping inflation. Experts are now debating whether the inflation rate for 1977 will be closer to 30 percent or 35 percent. In late September Madrid officially announced that consumer prices had risen by 3.1 percent in the month of July, bringing the inflation rate for the first seven months of this year to around 17 percent (nearly as high as all of 1976). Even according to the somewhat controversial government index, food prices rose by no less than 6 percent in that same month. Price controls, which do exist in theory, seem to be having little or no effect in practice.

The third crucial problem weighing on the Spanish economy is closely linked to the first two. It consists of growing unemployment and the precarious financial position of nationally important industrial enterprises.

Officially the present number of unemployed is given at about one million, or some 7.7 percent of the total labor force of 13 million (compared with an average of 2.3 percent in the years 1962-1973 and 2.8 percent in 1974). But it should be kept in mind that official working hours in Spain make it possible for many white-collar workers to pursue a second occupation (unregistered and untaxed) in the afternoon and evening. However, as soon as someone loses his main job he registers himself as unemployed in order to receive unemployment compensation, so that his actual financial situation may hardly deteriorate at all. Given these special circumstances, experts estimate the actual number of those totally dependent on government unemployment payments as no more than 600,000, which yields an unemployment rate of less than 5 percent, no higher than in other industrialized countries. Also ameliorating the situation is the fact that in Spain, as in Italy, unemployed industrial workers tend to remain in close contact with their rural relations, substantially increasing their ability to get along in crisis situations.

Nevertheless the flexibility of the Spanish economy in this respect should not be overestimated. Employing more than 33 percent of the total labor force, industry represents such a vital part of this country's productive strength that it seems incomprehensible to suggest artificially cutting back this sector's productivity, which is so crucial for exports. Yet precisely such a danger was raised last summer, when the government announced the introduction of credit restrictions as the only concrete flanking measure of the July 12 devaluation. Those restrictions caused a number of important enterprises to publicly state that liquidity difficulties would make it impossible for them to continue meeting their payrolls. It was little wonder, then, that in the course of September the Madrid securities market slumped to its lowest index level in decades and prominent industrial leaders literally began speaking of a situation "bordering on chaos."

Economic Changes Come Slowly

In view of these serious problem-complexes it is hardly surprising that, aside from those of the government itself, it is virtually impossible in Madrid these days to hear any optimistic views about the short- and medium-term prospects of the Spanish economy. The situation is further complicated by the fact that for some time to come—pessimists suggest a period of two years—the Cortes will be occupied with working out a new constitution. There is thus a real danger that, during this "legislative period," the government will be able to institute only relatively incoherent emergency measures of economic policy, such as repeated devaluations.

Aside from the abstinence from positive economic policy as a kind of misconstrued laissez-faire, the thing that Spanish economists emphasize in their criticisms of the Suárez regime's style of governing is its inexplicably long delay in creating the instruments and institutions necessary to formulate and execute economic policy at all. For example, Spain urgently needs a modern fiscal policy to help its economy toward health. But its tax system is outmoded, inefficient and extremely unfair, so that a thoroughgoing reform in this area is called for first. But such a task is not likely to be undertaken before a new constitution has been approved by the Cortes.

At the same time, responsible ministers are talking of the need for an income policy. But the free trade unions, who are supposed to function as partners in moderating the wage spiral, are only in the process of formation. And in this initial phase it is more popular to put forward maximum demands on the wage issue, in order to attract as many members as possible. Given this fact, it is difficult to see how the unions are to cooperate with the government on this important matter.

All in all, a preliminary survey of Spain's post-Franco evolution seems to yield the conclusion that the transition from the old, technocrat-controlled economic system to a market-oriented economic order may prove significantly more difficult than the democratization process on the political level. Yet critical observers in Madrid rightly point out that Spanish democracy can last only if the government succeeds soon enough in getting a grip on economic development.

SPAIN'S ECONOMIC CRISIS [3]

Spain is caught in what is considered its gravest economic crisis since the Civil War, and the country's newly democratic politics are taking on a sharper edge, with growing signs of polarization between the left and right.

    [3] From "Spain, With Its Economy in Crisis, Finds Itself Torn Politically, Too," by James M. Markham, special correspondent. New York *Times.* p 1A & 8A. Mr. 10, '78. © 1978 by The New York Times Company. Reprinted by permission.

Compounding the problems, the minority Government of Prime Minister Adolfo Suárez that emerged from last June's elections has not been able to gain the confidence of Spain's jittery financial class even though it has begun to move to the right. In searching for a larger constituency, Mr. Suárez has frightened the wealthy with talk of such things as a large income tax, but he has yet to give his center-right Union of the Democratic Center a firm popular base.

"Spain is at one of the most difficult moments in its history," warned Manuel Fraga Iribarne, the leader of the right-wing Popular Alliance, leaning intently from the podium of the high-domed Parliament building. He stirred little visible dissent among the legislators when he added somberly, "People may soon be calling us the sick man of Europe."

Grim economic realities have taken the euphoria out of Spanish politics. Big industries, internationally uncompetitive because of decades of protectionism, are tottering toward bankruptcy, hurt by a persistent recession in Europe, high labor costs and laws that make it difficult or costly to dismiss workers. Babcock & Wilcox Española, a huge equipment manufacturer in Bilbao, has gone into receivership. The Banco de Navarra collapsed and had to be rescued by the Bank of Spain, a fate that may soon befall five other small banks.

The largest automobile maker in Spain, Seat, has such a large inventory of cars that it wants to slash working time in its Barcelona plant dramatically. The Spanish steel industry may go almost a billion dollars into the red this year, and Altos Hornos del Mediterraneo, a large steel manufacturer in Valencia, is facing bankruptcy.

To avoid bankruptcy, thousands of companies have simply stopped making their social security contributions. The Government is now some $2.5 billion short in social security payments, which in Spain are a disguised form of taxation.

Feeling ignored in the higher councils of Mr. Suárez's Government, businessmen at the beginning of the year began organizing mass meetings and protests, accusing the Prime Minister of "economic treason." At the same time, some of Mr. Suárez's closest advisers, alarmed by the Government's slump in the opinion polls and signs of a big decline in investment, urged swift remedial action.

At the end of February, Mr. Suárez moved, dropping his unhappy Deputy Prime Minister for Economic Affairs, Enrique Fuentes Quintana, and four other economic ministers. A respected economics professor, Mr. Fuentes Quintana had trimmed the inflation rate impressively from an official 26.4 percent at the end of 1977 to what was looking like half of that this year and through devaluation of the peseta had improved a worrisome balance-of-payments situation.

Investors' Confidence Broken

But a tight money policy had broken the confidence of investors, unemployment had risen swiftly—more than a million Spaniards in a work force of 13.5 million do not have jobs—and Mr. Fuentes Quintana and his allies had further unsettled advocates of free enterprise by broaching the idea of nationalizing nuclear energy plants and electric power. The last straw was Mr. Fuentes Quintana's insistence on holding down agricultural prices, an affront to small farmers in central Spain whom Mr. Suárez perceives as his natural constituents.

To replace Mr. Fuentes Quintana, Mr. Suárez elevated a handful of uninspiring confidants, like himself longtime members of the upper reaches of government bureaucracy and, to appease business, brought in Agustín Rodríguez Sahagún, an outspoken entrepreneur and organizer of the anti-Government rallies, as Minister of Industry and Energy. "The middle classes and financial world slept better last night," asserted Abel Hernández, a pro-Government columnist, the morning after the Cabinet shuffle. Evidence suggests he was indulging in wishful thinking.

The strong men in the Cabinet are obscure, untested close friends of Mr. Suárez, and many politicians suspect that he will eventually be obliged to reach out to more established rightist figures, such as Mr. Fraga, to solidify his Government. The Popular Alliance's 16 seats in Parliament would be useful to the Prime Minister, who has only 165 seats in the 350-member lower house. Meanwhile, the Socialist Workers Party, the second strongest with 118 seats, is about to gain six by absorbing the small Popular Socialist Party.

Mr. Suárez is now expected to try to breathe some life into the economy and shore up ailing industries, keeping in mind the key municipal elections that are supposed to be held later this year. The Prime Minister's shaky Center Party has been trailing the Socialist Workers Party badly in opinion polls, and he has avoided setting a date to the irritation of both the Socialists and the Communists.

In leftist circles, there is talk of "mass mobilizations" to force the Government to call municipal elections by the summer. City halls across Spain are for the most part in the hands of holdover Francoists or men loyal to Mr. Suárez and the Prime Minister's opponents were exceptionally piqued when he picked a member of his own party to be Madrid's new mayor.

In another challenge the Socialists this week announced that they were pulling out of an all-party committee that has been working on a draft of a new constitution.

Government Loses a Vote

Mr. Fuentes Quintana was the architect of an all-party social pact aimed at checking inflation, largely through wage and price restraint. His departure has provoked accusations from the left that Mr. Suárez is about to renege on the pact to appease business. For the first time in Spain's young democracy, the Government this week was defeated in Parliament, by a vote of 159 to 134, as both the rightist Popular Alliance and the leftist parties declared its ambiguous explanation of the Cabinet shuffle "insufficient."

This slap at Mr. Suárez was only one measure of the sharpening tone of political discourse—"the end of the politics of consensus," in the words of Javier Solana, a Socialist Member of Parliament. In Parliament, the Socialists openly accused high-ranking members of the governing party of corruption in the forging of a controversial fishing agreement with Morocco.

Union elections now under way are for the first time giving the Communists and Socialists defined constituencies, which will be more difficult to control as unemployment spreads. Abandoning Madrid's salon politics, Santiago Carrillo, the Communist leader, appeared at a huge demonstration in the northern city of Aviles to protest proposed layoffs at a steel plant. In backward Andalusia, unemployed agricultural workers staged "symbolic" occupations of five large estates.

"I am terrified we are going to have one and a half million unemployed next year," said José Ramón Lasuén, an economic adviser to the Prime Minister.

At bottom Mr. Suárez's problem is that his overriding priority is to get Parliament to write a constitution that will enshrine the position of his friend and leader, King Juan Carlos. To do this, he must avoid too sharp a lurch to his natural constituency on the right, which would break the fragile political consensus and, just possibly, stir questions about the monarchy.

But this priority, at a time of deep economic crisis, conflicts with a need to build both investor confidence and a sure basis for a party that would broadly represent the Spanish upper and middle classes.

"Prime Minister Suárez should be representing the civilized right, the businessmen and so on," observed Mr. Solana, the Socialist legislator. "But he has not been able to do so. It is a Government that is a little bit in the air."

PAYING INCOME TAXES IN SPAIN [4]

Leaning slightly over the gold cutlery, the Spanish businessman smiled slyly at Treasury Minister Francisco [Fernández] Ordoñez, and turned to the countess seated across the table.

"Well," said the businessman, glancing out toward the hostess's swimming pool, "I would say that, with the house, the swimming pool, the furniture and the other goods, net wealth could be put at approximately. . . ." The guests broke into light laughter.

The subject was a novel one in Spain: paying income taxes.

In the last year, this country has made important strides toward becoming a democratic state. Now, in the vaulted recesses of the Treasury Ministry, a band of young economists and technocrats is putting together what could be the most ambitious reform of Prime Minister Adolfo Suárez's centrist Government to date.

That great, necessary nightmare of Western industrial civilization, the income tax, is about to descend in earnest on Spaniards—at a time when their economy is in a state of crisis, with savings at low levels and disinvestment spreading throughout industry.

"I can't say that all the people have put themselves at peace with the Lord in this matter," said José Victor Sevilla, the Director General of Taxation. "But there certainly has been a jump forward. Before, income-tax evasion was the first national sport in this country, even ahead of soccer."

Mr. Sevilla is a genial, 35-year-old economist and, if the Government and parliament permit him, he will oversee a genuine collection of income taxes, armed with a newly mobilized data bank and some 1,500 tax inspectors who by next year should see their ranks increase to 2,500.

Laws already on the books will permit inspectors, in

[4] From "A Western Burden, Paying Income Tax, Looms in Spain," by James M. Markham, Madrid correspondent. New York Times. p 61 & 72. My. 11, '78. © 1978 by The New York Times Company. Reprinted by permission.

special cases, to look at citizens' bank accounts and after trial, send big-time tax dodgers to jail—unheard of in Franco's Spain.

"People think that the machinery we have works less well than it really does," said Mr. Sevilla. But he acknowledges that his countrymen have not in the past taken the tax man seriously. "This is not Colombia, but neither is it the United States. You know what I would like to see in Spain? The scenes you see in American movies where the guy grabbed by the cop, says, 'Watch out, I'm a taxpayer.' "

That may take a while.

More Equitable Burden Sought

Spain's first income-tax law went on the books in 1932 under the short-lived Second Republic, but the Franco regime collected only payroll, or withholding, taxes from salaried workers while huge stretches of the middle and upper classes paid hardly any taxes at all—and the very rich paid even less.

Now, by lowering the taxation rates to levels below the rest of Western Europe, Mr. Sevilla and his men hope to collect more revenue and make the tax burden fall more equitably across Spain's social spectrum.

A Government-proclaimed amnesty on past fraudulent returns has induced some 175,000 families to "regularize" their standing with the tax authorities, with no questions asked.

"I think that most Spaniards have come around to the idea that they should pay taxes," said Mr. Ordoñez, the Treasury Minister, who has made tax reform the centerpiece of his labors.

Like many things the reformist Government is doing, the income-tax law could boomerang against Mr. Suárez's own middle-class electoral constituency. The average industrial worker will not be paying more taxes, but self-employed professionals and corporate executives will. Moreover, the very rich will still find themselves, by world standards, lightly taxed, with plenty of legal loopholes to reduce their burdens.

Under the Government's proposals, a married couple with two children with an annual income of the equivalent of $25,000 a year will be taxed at a rate of 16 percent; a similar couple with an income of $62,500 rises to a bracket of 26 percent, but, at $125,000 the rate is only 39 percent.

Mr. Ordoñez has been obliged to anticipate one of the most trenchant criticisms of the income tax, which was raised by the liberal Madrid daily *El País* in a recent editorial.

"Where is our tax money going?" asked the newspaper. "In other European countries, there are high taxes, but the highways, hospitals, housing and schooling, for example, are infinitely superior."

The newspaper hardly needed to remind its readers that most Spaniards have to pay to get their children educated, that the bloated social security service, whose budget is as large as the state's, is inefficient and corrupt or that the government subsidizes a range of crippled industries that, in some cases, have been dumped on it by skittish business-men.

The Treasury Minister insists that a new law on the control of public expenditure will soon be passed, so citizens can know where their tax money is in fact going. The new taxes will probably not begin to bite until next year—when their political impact will start to be felt as well.

"There is no fiscal conscience in this country," said an adviser to Prime Minister Suárez. "People do have a kind of moral disposition to pay taxes. What they don't know yet is what kind of a trap they are about to fall into."

III. THE SPANISH SOCIAL AND CULTURAL SCENE

EDITOR'S INTRODUCTION

The social and cultural scene in Spain is being greatly influenced by the recent political and economic changes in that nation. Population movement to the cities and urban crime are two comparatively new problems that Spaniards must face. At the same time, peasants of the countryside gain self-assurance as democracy takes deeper roots in rural areas. Spain, long equated with the most conservative Catholicism, also now finds the church greatly waning in influence. These are the principal developments discussed in this section. In the first article, Arnold Hottinger, a *Neue Zürcher Zeitung* (Zurich) correspondent for Spain and the Arab countries, sketches the broader themes of Spanish cultural history in this century. Then James M. Markham, a special correspondent of the New York *Times*, reports on the flight to the cities and the growing urban crime problem. Professor David D. Gregory of Dartmouth College, an expert on southern Spain, discusses the emergence of political consciousness and greater democracy in the rural areas of Spain. The changing role of the Catholic church is dealt with by Merle Linda Wolin, a free-lance journalist who is writing a biography of La Pasionaria, the most admired and most hated orator of the Spanish Civil War. The final article in this section, on Spanish political refugees from Franco's Spain, is by Nancy Macdonald, director of Spanish Refugee Aid, Inc.

SPANISH CULTURE IN THIS CENTURY [1]

Spanish culture in the twentieth century began with a process of self-discovery and self-portrayal. The so-called

[1] Article by Arnold Hottinger, the *Neue Zürcher Zeitung*'s correspondent for Spain and the Arab countries. *Swiss Review of World Affairs*. 27:19-23. D. '77. Reprinted by permission.

Generation of '98—the generation that began its intellectual life under the influence of the great defeat of Cuba [the Spanish-American War] which put an end to the Spanish Empire—took upon itself the task of rediscovering Spain for itself and for all Spaniards. Castile is one of the major themes of that period in prose, poetry and painting. The Generation of '98 read "Don Quijote" with new eyes and gave it a new interpretation, seeing it as symbolizing the constant search for the Hispanic essence. The writer Azorin found that essence in the landscape and gave eloquent expression to its silences and its shimmering expanse. In his works individual characters are merely products of the Castilian village countryside or the plains of La Mancha, personified bits of earth, so to speak. Miguel de Unamuno also pursued that elusive essence in his essays, always paradoxical, always surprising, full of an incorruptible originality, as though he were trying to surprise and capture "the Castilian" through intellectual acrobatics. Machado, the greatest of modern Spanish poets, linked his personal fate so closely to that of the landscape of Soria, on the upper Duero, that today it is difficult to see the poplars of those high plains except through his eyes.

The undertaking of the people of '98 was a turning back from cosmopolitan Hispanicity and its political confusions to the stillness of the Meseta, the Spanish interior, and the search for the innermost contents which nourished the soul of Spain and the Spaniards. At the end of that search, inevitably, came the encounter with God—a God who was revealed as distinctly Spanish and not particularly Catholic, a divinity who, for Unamuno as well as Machado, was made manifest in the paradox of mortality: He was present, precisely because all else was transient.

Out of that search for the innermost essence of Spain grew a kind of Silver Age of Spanish culture, second only to the Golden Age of the sixteenth century. The Spanish phenomenon stands out from the European panorama of the years before and immediately after World War I like primal rock before a backdrop of brick houses. Nationalism in both cases, of course: But in the case of Spain it involved a probing, critical and sometimes ironic view of one's own essence and fate, triggered by defeat and by the pressing challenge of a rising tide of positivism among the then so self-assured Americans and Europeans. In the case of those "others," as Unamuno called them, nationalism was based rather on a superficial sense of having accomplished so much, a sense that was to be violently disrupted by the chaos of the postwar era.

In Spain that first meditative and self-analytical generation, the founding fathers of the country's contemporary culture, was followed by a second group, known as the Generation of '27 [a group of outstanding Spanish romantic poets]—more cheerful, playful, more brilliant, with the urbanity and richness of ideas of an Ortega y Gasset, the guitar-like vibrations of a García Lorca. A certain rootedness and solidity seemed to have been provided by the older generation, so that the younger could flourish in that soil, could thrive and be more cosmopolitan, more alive to and participating in the currents of the world, though always with an unmistakably Spanish tone.

The poet-playwright García Lorca traveled to New York, the painter Picasso to Paris. For the first time since the Renaissance Spain had schools of worldwide renown (the *Institución de Libre Enseñanza*), its universities blossomed and provided settings for a number of outstanding masters of the humanities (Menendez Pidal, Damaso Alonso, Americo Castro and many more).

The Effects of the Civil War

The Spanish Civil war broke in upon all this like a storm from a clear and serene sky . . . though perhaps it had not been so very serene after all. There had been warning signs, social tensions, widespread poverty, activist workers, class-obsessed officers whose mentality stemmed from the North African colonial wars, an unresolved agrarian problem, a temporary dictatorship. Yet all of that is hardly enough to explain the civil war, especially considering that Spain kept out of World War I and, unlike Italy and Germany, cannot be said to have derived its susceptibility to fascism from the consequences of that conflict.

The roots of the Spanish catastrophe, which broke out in the midst of a period of cultural blossoming, have not yet been completely uncovered. A study of all the available documents from that period indicates that the Church must have played a key role in a manner which seems almost incomprehensible from today's perspective. In the prewar years pro-Church and anti-Church forces were aligned in sharp mutual hostility. There was also a cultural world, which had largely turned its back on that dogmatic antagonism and accepted the possibility of coexistence between an introverted Catholicism on the one hand and a humanitarian theism, pantheism or even atheism on the other hand. But in the streets there was a brutal clash between the clericalism and anti-clericalism inherent in the old Hispanic legacy—and during the period of pre-civil war unrest many churches were set aflame.

The fact that the cultural elite of that time was so removed from the harsh realities of the fanatically-inclined street mobs indicates certain weaknesses in the cultural renaissance of the period. Was it superficial? Was it too far ahead of the rest of the country and thus cut off from it?— *"No es eso!"* ("This isn't it!") was the famous cry of Ortega, an old advocate of the Republic, when the Republic had been proclaimed. And that was the reaction of all Spain's true intellectuals toward the civil war. There was an inevitable fright and revulsion at the Goyaesque abyss which suddenly opened before them. Some contented themselves with the observation: "That's how we Spaniards are!"

For Americo Castro the question of "Why?" became the focal point of all his later work. It prompted him to probe with his acute intellect the convention-masked depths of Spanish history and society . . . Today one can only venture the suspicion that the Castilian essence which the Generation of '98 believed to have found in the landscape, the prototypes and the unchanging roots of *la raza*, the "race," must have had a largely unrecognized historical background which was linked not to the Meseta but to the old life-style and social forms of the Spaniards, their churches and anti-churches, their *bandos* (fanatical groups) and castes. The traditional mentality must have formed a kind of amalgam with modern class-consciousness, class theories and class struggle, in the center of which stood the old, mighty institution of the Spanish Church. The Church became a symbol around which differences of opinion crystallized, and the symbol was often confused with the purpose of the struggle. When churches were set afire, it was the old Spanish society that was meant. A crusade was carried out, which in reality served to protect the interests of certain segments of Spanish society.

The Era of Censorship

Spain's culture suffered severely from the civil war and perhaps even more from its consequences. Preprint censorship for all printed materials lasted until 1966, followed by another 10 years of post-print censorship for books, newspapers and journals, which forced authors to exercise self-censorship. The intellectual elite fled at first, and later emigrated. University life was harnessed to the political goals of the dictatorship and for more than a decade professors were selected on the basis of their political reliability. There was a long period when only a narrow Spanish version of neo-Thomism was given official sanction as philosophy at university level.

Even those intellectuals who had sided with the Nationalists during the civil war began to feel themselves inner or outer expatriates as the Franco regime came to concentrate increasingly on consolidating its privileges and privileged classes. In the postwar years a wide gulf opened between a democratic Europe and a totalitarian Spain whose ancient pride was exploited to counter the external boycott with an inner isolation.

But Spain's spiritual and intellectual life never succumbed entirely to the totalitarian nature of the Franco state. Since the start of the Inquisition (1478 A.D.) the Spaniards have known how to write books that slip through the nets of the censors. (Important aspects of "Don Quijote" are probably due to that knowledge.) And always, alongside of totalitarian intent, there was a Mediterranean easygoingness which the finest spirits expanded into tolerance. Ties of family and friendship proved stronger than orders from above and the transparent imperatives of "empire."

With painstaking effort the Spaniards gathered together the pieces of their shattered intellectual life and somehow carried it onward. But the first fruits of more-than-provincial nature did not ripen until about 20 years after the civil war. In the literary field it was the appearance of *"Tiempo de Silencio"* ("Time of Silence") by Luis Martin-Santos in 1964 that marked a reconnection with major accomplishments in contemporary world literature. But significant works had appeared even earlier (by Cela, Sanchez Ferlosio, etc.), and the continuation of Spanish literature in exile constituted a second stream of qualitatively equal importance. Roman Sender's masterpiece *"Cronica del Alba,"* as well as the most important Spanish poetry since the civil war, that of Cernuda, appeared abroad, as did the poems of Leon Felipe, which remained banned in Spain until relatively recently. Spain's universities, too, needed the rest of the world in order to keep up with current science and developments in the humanities. Their existence remained precarious, partly throttled by the political agitation of the last two decades, but things began looking up when Spaniards began traveling once more and students began receiving scholarships for studies abroad.

The Effects of Industrialization

In the economic realm the last 15 of Franco's 39 years brought a decisive shift for Spain, which could not fail to have an effect on the country's intellectual life. With foreign financial and technical help, the land entered a major phase of industrialization. Its face changed swiftly and fundamentally. Today it is no longer a nation of leisurely meditation on the upper level nor of mob battles in the streets. Spanish society has become more coherent. On weekends thousands of automobiles ride out into the countryside and return on Sunday evening, as they do in all other cities of Europe and North America. Nearly all Spaniards have now become "consumers," which has awakened new intellectual needs and new questions. They want to know more about their own society, about how its complex mechanisms work and why. There is little belief any longer in the fundamental truths of "la raza" which make of each and every Spaniard something different and unique. Even the Church has ceased playing the role of the old Spanish standard-bearer of the crusades against the Moors and other heretics. Between the Second Vatican Council and the year 1971, when the new ideas finally triumphed at the Bishops' Conference, the Spanish Church went through a quiet but thoroughgoing revolution which brought it to the point of wanting to separate itself from the state as much as possible; today its dominant trend is to stand with the opposition rather than be the *Ecclesia triumphans*, to share the suffering of the oppressed rather than share the power of the rulers.

The Spaniards have come closer to Europe. An important role in that process of adjustment has been played by the shift of population away from the villages and small towns of the Meseta and toward the coastal areas. This took place parallel to a reawakening of the country's various linguistic subcultures, Galician, Basque, Catalan, which today can make a justified claim to being more vital and creative than the Castilian. These geographically peripheral cultures also serve as mediators and links to Europe, Catalan most effectively, of course, but the other two as well with their connections to France, England and Portugal. *Lo castizo*, Castilian, is of little interest on the periphery of the Iberian Peninsula; in fact, it is even perceived as hostile. The new and burgeoning industrial society there is searching to discover its own laws. There is a growing sociological literature, analysis instead of meditation, books of political, sociological and psychological investigation; there are films which are also of an analytical nature; difficult novels, alternating between the unconscious of individuals and movements within the collective psyche (Benet, Luis and Juan Goytisolo); abstract painting; experimental theater . . . All these things are part of the new Spanish society, more flexible, more extraverted, restless and questing, pluralistic, multiform and multilingual, a society which for a long time was fermenting beneath the crust of Spain's aging dictatorship and which is now pushing out toward the light of day.

THE FLIGHT TO SPAIN'S CITIES [2]

The population of Fuentelfresno, a cluster of sagging stone houses, barns and a derelict church huddled on a low plateau, is two. If Félix García, wind-tanned farmer, and his wife move out, Fuentelfresno will become an abandoned village, one of hundreds such across Spain.

"If I do not die soon, I will move," said Mr. García with a grin that seemed a kind of private joke with his deity. "I am about to complete my 59th year."

Against the spectacular backdrop of the snow-wrapped Sierra del Moncayo, his shaggy white dog yapped at the feet of a flock of skittish sheep.

Seven years ago, a census in this somber stretch of Old Castile found that there were 22 people in Fuentelfresno, a far cry from the 200 who lived here when Félix García was born, though enough to call a community. But the steady hemorrhaging of its population continued, with more lucrative jobs and better schooling in Zaragoza, Barcelona and Frankfurt drawing its sons away.

"More left than died," said Plácido García, resting a mud-caked shovel on his shoulder. Félix García's 30-year-old son farms the family's wheat and barley fields in the mornings and in the evenings works as a bartender in the nearby provincal capital of Soria.

[2] From "Flight to Cities Empties Spain's Countryside," by James M. Markham, Madrid correspondent. New York *Times.* p 2A. Mr. 29, '78. © 1978 by The New York Times Company. Reprinted by permission.

"A man who is married, he cannot work the land," he said. "To live here with a family is impossible because there are no schools. Six years ago, there was a school here, but then it closed. Three years ago, when I married, I left the village. Two years ago, the last family with children left."

"I can remember when I was young here," he said, squinting in the bright winter sun. "There were 30 or 40 kids here and we had a good time."

The flight from the land has occurred throughout Europe, but in Spain it has come with a wrenching, brutal swiftness, telescoping into years what took decades elsewhere. In 1950, half the nation's active population was employed in agriculture; today 22 percent are. From 1960 to 1975 two million Spaniards left the country in search of work and over five million abandoned the countryside for Spanish cities.

Spain's population of 36 million is more than double that of 1900, but seven of the country's 50 provinces, including Soria, have fewer people today than they did at the turn of the century. Twenty-three provinces have registered population decreases since 1950, when Spain's efforts to become an industrialized nation began in earnest.

Money Goes to the Cities

The Franco dictatorship's concentration on industrial development turned Spanish agriculture into the economy's neglected stepchild. Credit and even rural savings were funneled into Madrid, Barcelona and Bilbao, while agricultural policy consisted largely of price-support mechanisms that discouraged crop diversification and kept yields among the lowest in Western Europe. The advent of democracy has not changed things in the countryside.

An amphitheater of high land girdled by mountains, Soria [province] supported 150,000 people, mostly villagers, in 1900, but today has fewer than 90,000 inhabitants. In 1900, the town of Soria had only 7,000 residents; today 28,000 people live there and almost 10,000 live in two other biggish towns. The countryside looks, and feels, empty.

"Soria is going to become a desert," lamented Carmelo Romero, a 27-year-old historian, standing before a map pinpointing the 273 villages, or pueblos, in the province that have fewer than 100 inhabitants. "The average age in the pueblos is about 50. It is almost an archeological collection of old people who know they are doomed to die there. They all live 10 months for the two months in summer when their children bring the grandchildren."

The abandonment of the countryside has meant the closing of many churches, and conservative Sorians were shocked last fall when José Luis Souto, the head of a group interested in preserving the province's artistic patrimony, charged that the bishopric in Burgo de Osma was selling ecclesiastical treasures. "They are converting Soria into a land without roots," said Mr. Souto angrily, likening the brisk sale of church art to "Chicago in the 1930s." Robberies have denuded other churches.

Little has been done to stem the loss of people—there are more Sorians living in nearby Zaragoza than in Soria Province—though there has been talk of setting up small farm-area industries that would create new jobs. "All the villages cannot be saved," said Marcos Molinero, the bearded editor of a local weekly. "It is necessary to save the big ones."

Last September Félix Pastor Ridruejo, a wealthy notary public who heads the rightist Popular Alliance in Soria, brought together several longtime Israeli kibbutz people with young Sorians whom he hoped to interest in a self-sustaining agricultural commune that might serve as a model for future development.

But he found it difficult to translate a free-floating, slightly anarchist sentiment among the young into a commitment to do hard agricultural work. The idea of a "return to the land," popular in the United States, has not taken hold among Spain's citified young.

Houses Are Deserted

"What? Young people?" asked an astonished 47-year-old woman in the village of Pedraza, which has a population of

24. "The youngest people are us." She and her husband, a soft-spoken 51-year-old farmer named Julián la Mata, make up two-thirds of Pedraza's able-bodied residents. They have to send their 12-year-old son to a state-run boarding school in Soria, where he lives with other rural children as young as six.

"When he comes here on the weekends, he has no one to play with," said Mrs. La Mata. "It's sad."

Smoking a hand-rolled cigarette, her husband conceded he might be the last man to farm this gray stubbly land. "Now our son is going into another environment," he said. "It will cost him to come back."

Down the road, in the village of La Rubia, Bonifacio Gómez, a grizzled 70-year-old, stood by a splashing fountain and pointed out the stone buildings that had once housed the village priest and the school teacher. Both are deserted. A priest comes occasionally on Sundays to say mass.

"See what a pretty school it was," said Mr. Gómez with a doleful gesture toward another disused building.

"Twenty years ago you should have seen this pueblo—everybody with their flocks, with 100 people living here. Now there are 16. I have four kids, all outside: two in Barcelona, one in Logroño, the other in San Sebastián. How can I keep my kids here—my four kids? Nobody wants to come and live in the pueblos, not the priest, not anybody."

SPAIN'S DEMOCRATIC COUNTRYSIDE [3]

A surprising change has taken place in the political mood of Spain's rural areas in the past 12 months.

Historically the Spanish countryside was politically dormant. The peasants and landless day laborers were alienated from the cities where liberal, republican doctrines took root.

The ruling conservative upper class—manipulating the

[3] From "Democracy Takes Root in Spain's Countryside," by David D. Gregory, professor at Dartmouth College, and an expert on southern Spain. *Christian Science Monitor.* p 16. D. 14, '77. Reprinted by permission from *The Christian Science Monitor.* © 1977 The Christian Science Publishing Society. All rights reserved.

rural masses' passivity and estrangement from the cities—was provided with a reliable source of votes, laborers, and soldiers to resist the reform programs of the more progressive elements of urban Spanish society.

The rural exodus of the twentieth century began to weaken the conservatives' power base. In 1900, cities of more than 20,000 still accounted for less than 21 percent of Spain's total population. By 1977 the figure had risen to more than 55 percent.

Only in the last 15 years, however, has there been a significant interchange between migrants and nonmigrants, bringing the city and its ideologies of reform closer to the countryside.

During the weeks preceding Spain's national referendum on constitutional reforms in December last year, the peasants and day laborers in the South ingratiated themselves by asking the local elites how they should vote and by breaking illegal strikes initiated by a minority of fellow workers.

Forty years of local despotism under the Franco regime and unequal access to scarce jobs administered by the wealthy made the rural masses cautious.

But this past September, barely three months after Spain's parliamentary elections, this writer was struck not so much by the evaporation of fear in southern Spain as by its transference from the laboring classes to the rural upper class who seemed on the verge of panic.

Rafael Cabezas, a large landowner, said: "We now are the wicked ones; those considered harmful to society . . . and all the people who were nothing before have a new moral strength. How can it be possible that we who have been good for 40 years suddenly became the bad ones? We have not changed."

Newfound Self-Assurance

Today the working class talks publicly with a newfound self-assurance based on the fact that throughout southern Spain the Socialist Workers Party (Partido Socialista Obrera Español or PSOE) headed by Felipe González was the victor in the June 15 legislative elections with over 39 percent of the total vote.

The major change in political consciousness actually occurred during the three weeks preceding the elections when men from the cities—many who had once lived in the rural towns—returned to the countryside and campaigned vigorously. They tore down the 40 years of the Franco dictatorship and accused Prime Minister Adolfo Suárez of being the leader of a false party of the center (Union de Centro Democratico or UCD), which they termed a mere extension of the Franco past.

The people listened and waited for the Civil Guard to arrest the outsiders for their outspokenness. That they were allowed to talk openly and leave the town without repercussions had a far greater impact than the content of their political speeches.

By the time the elections arrived, 19 parties had established themselves in the towns, in the rural regions, usually through the efforts of the local schoolteachers. Representing parties on both the left and the right, the teachers used covert lists of local men killed by either the fascists or the communists in the Civil War to open old wounds and enlist the active support of their families.

The real key to change in the rural areas, however, lies not in the political parties but in the newly established labor unions. During the Franco regime there was one national, vertical syndicate throughout Spain that represented all workers and employers, established wages and set prices.

On last July 1 the Spanish workers were finally freed from mandatory membership in the syndicate, and clandestine groups, like the Communist workers' commissions (Comisiones Obreras) and the Socialist Federation of Workers of the Land, were allowed to recruit members legally. In many of the towns there now are four to five unions competing for workers' support.

A problem with the profusion of political parties and unions in the rural areas is that there are not a sufficient number of educated people to make these new institutions work effectively. The organizers behind the unions are returned migrant workers from France and West Germany who have been exposed to other West European labor movements.

A great deal of confusion still exists because the new free labor unions are free in every sense except to enter into direct collective bargaining with employers—a right the government has retained, but which the workers ignore.

Unemployment in southern Spain is the highest it has been in a decade (more than 15 percent). Yet the men who filled many town streets in Andalusia during this writer's visit were on strike. September and October are months when intensive labor is needed to harvest edible olives.

The workers had been unemployed since late spring, but they were refusing to go to the fields. They wanted a daily wage of 1,300 pesetas ($15.76) and were not pacified by a new government regulation raising the minimum daily wage to 500 pesetas ($6.06) beginning October 1, 1977. Their other demands were: to work a seven-hour day, to allow no one to work overtime and take jobs away from others, to make sure women receive the same wages as men, and to insure that laborers be contracted for work in the new union centers rather than from the streets or the bars by landowners' foremen.

To reinforce these demands, the men forced the commercial establishments, except for the pharmacies and bakeries, to close down for 24 hours.

Antonio Fernández, a worker, said: "What do we have to lose? I have only been able to work here 12 days since February. I went to Barcelona looking for a job. But there all the small businesses are cutting back or going bankrupt. . . . I had to come back home. Now they want me to work for two months. If I do . . . they are going to have to pay so my family can live during the months when there is no work. The landowners say that we are unreasonable and are destroying production and that we must help the government solve its economic problems. What do their problems have to do with my family's problems?"

A group of town officials complained that Spain's "liberty" was only "libertinism." What they felt was needed was another tough little general with a sword in his hand. They were particularly upset because the striking workers had earlier marched on the courthouse demanding that the mayor immediately distribute the unemployment benefits that he had received from the provincial governor. The mayor refused to release the funds to support the workers' strike.

Mayor Describes Problem

In describing his problem the mayor said: "Manual labor has become too costly. I am not surprised to see the landowners pull out all their olive trees to substitute crops like wheat and sunflowers which require fewer men."

The fact remains that local officials in the towns and cities are politically appointed holdovers from the Franco regime who are likely to lose their posts during the municipal elections due to be held early in 1978. Therefore, most of the local governing bodies are working against the liberalization of the countryside initiated by Prime Minister Suárez and democratically elected representatives in Madrid.

Their tactics are to discredit the fledgling attempts at democracy. First, it is increasingly difficult to get enough of the councilmen together to form a quorum to transact local government business. Second, all cash reserves are being spent so as to leave the incoming mayor and councilmen with nothing but outstanding debts. Third, all municipal services are being cut back—especially sanitation—to give an impression of decline.

Finally, the police, in the cities as well as the towns, have been instructed to use greater tolerance in dealing with petty criminals and juvenile delinquents by letting them back out on the streets after a night in jail, thus promoting a climate of fear among the local citizenry. Every attempt is made to elevate the Franco years of "union, order, and peace" above the chaotic present caused by doctrines of "autonomy, justice, and liberty."

It is heartening to see that political change has finally reached the countryside. But, democracy is going to need a healthier climate of economic stability, if it is to survive.

Inflation which began at 20 percent this year will close at 30 percent. The $4 billion trade deficit, the precipitous decline of the stock market, and the alarming number of bankruptcies have halted investment. The spiral of unemployment ascends monthly. This fall and winter 798 new labor pacts have to be negotiated in order to avoid a series of strikes that would affect 358,764 managers and more than 2,272,072 workers.

The danger is that unless the centralist party of Mr. Suárez, with the direct cooperation of the Socialists, begins to solve the nation's economic problems, the country could be pushed toward the extremes it has avoided to date. In this scenario many of those who voted for the UCD would move further toward the right, while those who supported the PSOE would move toward more radical forms of socialism.

SPAIN'S SOARING URBAN CRIME [4]

Cathedrals in Oviedo and Murcia are robbed of precious treasures. Muggers and thieves multiply their depredations. Illegal gamblers operate openly on Barcelona's gracious Ramblas. Convicts riot and burn their prisons, and a left-wing senator, himself a priest, says they should all get amnesty. Pornography floods the newsstands.

Many Spaniards are troubled that their new democratic order has brought with it a wave of permissiveness and crime.

"Now, and in a growing manner, the city streets—and those of Barcelona, in particular—are flooded with threats of burglary, holdups and rape," the conservative Barcelona newspaper *La Vanguardia* said in an editorial. "Bands of

[4] From "Soaring Urban Crime Troubling Spaniards," by James M. Markham, Madrid correspondent. New York *Times*. p 16. D. 18, '77. © 1977 by The New York Times Company. Reprinted by permission.

delinquents, mostly young, are violently and cruelly grabbing everything they can put their hands on."

Manuel Fraga Iribarne, chief of the right-wing Popular Alliance, commented: "This is a serious crisis of public order. We are not being given all the facts, but it is obvious that the incidence of rape, robbery and violence of all kinds is increasing dramatically."

Though there is no doubt that crime, particularly armed robbery, is growing, it is uncertain how much this has to do with the political liberalization. Interior Ministry statistics show that burglaries and holdups jumped 44 percent, from 41,054 to 59,234, between 1975, when Francisco Franco died, and 1976, when King Juan Carlos began nudging Spain along democratic paths. In the first six months of this year, according to the same nationwide figures, there were 36,010 such crimes, which, projected for all of 1977, would represent another jump of almost 22 percent over last year.

On the other hand the statistics show 111 murders and homicides, a relatively stable and extremely low number. February in Spain was without a murder—something that can rarely be said about a day in New York, with a fifth of the population.

The statistics may generally be viewed with a jaundiced eye, but what is certain is that an unshackled press writes freely about crime in the streets these days, whereas under the Franco dictatorship it was obliged to portray a country at peace with itself. The change is a bit of a shock.

Diario 16, a lively Madrid paper, has been running a well-read series on crime in the capital, district by district, that suggests that more and more thugs are getting guns. It has found that the capital has an exotic variety of criminals, ranging from relatively harmless gamberros, who like to pinch amorous couples in Retiro Park, to trigger-happy chorizos—literally sausages—who murdered a hotel clerk during a robbery in October.

"In comparison with other countries, we are still a lot lower," Pedro Herranz Rosado, head of the 130-member

Madrid Criminal Brigade, told a visitor. "Not so violent as France or Italy or your country—we haven't got there yet."

Reflection of Population Rise

Mr. Herranz, who joined the brigade in 1947, when it was roughly the same size it is today, sees only a glancing connection between the advent of democracy and the rise in crime. His view is that crime is growing steadily and naturally, just as Madrid has grown from a city of 800,000 when he joined to four million today.

Like policemen elsewhere, he feels that he is combating a festering and growing pool of recidivists—the statistics tend to bear him out—so he laments both the elimination of a law that permitted him to hold suspected pickpockets 28 days and the clogging of a criminal-justice system that, like New York's, seems unable to function fast enough.

He also remarked that Spain's growing contacts with the outside world had brought sophistication to the criminal sector.

"A lot of South American criminals—Argentinians, Chileans, Peruvians—have been expelled from their own countries and have come here. We expel them when we catch them, but they come back on false passports," he explained. "And a lot of our people have learned outside, too. We had a Spaniard, a pickpocket, and he went to Brussels and started robbing banks. He learned that there."

Under the Franco regime the police were heavily politicized and spent as much time snooping around for Communists as they did hunting common criminals, a habit that is just beginning to change. "We must return tranquillity and confidence to Spanish families in the face of aggression and crime, to businessmen in the face of burglaries and holdups," Interior Minister Rodolfo Martin Villa told a recent gathering of policemen.

As in other cities where there are outcries against rises in crime, the Government has responded with a measure that is sure to be popular. Beginning in February serenos, or nightwatchmen, will return to the streets of major cities,

6,000 in the capital alone. Withdrawn in March 1976 as an economy measure, they will come back in strength—this time armed with pistols.

SPAIN'S CHANGING CHURCH [5]

Spain, it would seem, is no longer a Catholic country.

The idea that it is, says Spanish social activist E. Miret Magdalena, "should be done away with once and for all. Most Spanish people are not and haven't been Catholic for a long time. The church dominated our lives for the past 40 years only because of Franco's regime. It was coercion. And now, without the support of the government or the Spanish people, the church is in total crisis. It's completely lost its identity."

E. Miret Magdalena, a religious man and former president of Spain's once powerful Catholic worker organization, *Accion Catolica*, has been predicting the demise of the church since 1960. And he hasn't been alone. An increasing number of priests, bishops, government leaders and academicians echo Magdalena's contention, pointing out that only the dictorial protection of *El Generalisimo* gave the Catholic Church its extraordinary power in Spanish life.

In his 1976 book, *La Revolucion de lo Religioso*, Magdalena claims that only 15 percent to 20 percent of the country's 35 million inhabitants now practice Catholicism.

Most Spaniards, weary of fascism and autocratic rule, identify the Catholic Church with the same forces of government repression being dismantled since Franco's death in 1975. According to Magdalena, Franco's power allowed the Spanish ecclesiastical hierarchy to disregard widespread religious disillusionment, because the church neither looked to nor depended upon popular support.

Now, however, the Vatican and the recent democratically elected government are working to modernize the

[5] From "Like Spain, Its Church Must Change—or Perish," by Merle Linda Wolin, a free-lance journalist. Los Angeles *Times*. p 2 IV. F. 5, '78. Copyright 1978, Los Angeles Times. Los Angeles Times/Washington Post News Service. Reprinted with permission.

Concordat, the official pact between the Spanish church and the state. These negotiations, which should produce a new church-state agreement by April, are forcing the Spanish Catholic Church to confront the scars of national despair and oppression suffered throughout the Franco years. A basic ecclesiastical challenge now confronts the church: It must develop a new form of Catholicism, one capable of surviving without the theocratic support of a dictatorship.

But the church has become a house divided. Conflicting factions within that institution range from some fascist bishops who, comparing Franco to the Emperor Charlemagne, propose canonizing him as a saint, to a growing number of Communist priests who view the implementation of Marxism as the only way to attain Christian values in modern Spain.

The vast majority of Spanish bishops waver between the two factions, espousing human rights while seeking to preserve their entrenched privileges. Almost all, however, agree that something drastic must be done to stem the rising tide of popular disinterest and anticlericalism afflicting the Spanish church.

Anticlerical sentiments, however, are hardly new to Spain. In the turbulent years preceding the Spanish Civil War, convents and monasteries were often set on fire by landless peasants and political militants who knew that if the democratic forces failed to win, the church would help elevate fascism to power. Religious icons were symbolically "executed," even while thousands of Franco's clerical supporters died in battles between democratic and fascist forces.

When Franco assumed the reins of leadership in 1939, the church was well rewarded for its faithful support. In exchange for granting Franco complete power to choose the country's ruling bishops, the Spanish church became the sole guardian of official Spanish values and morals. The church censored the press and the film industry, then seized control of the entire educational system, including teachers and textbooks.

Catholic representatives, moreover, sat on virtually every

legislative council in the country, and no laws were made without their prior approval. Divorce and abortion were quickly abolished. Spaniards looking for work often had to produce baptismal certificates before being hired. Catholic priests became exempt from military duty and criminal prosecution in civil courts. Throughout the Franco years, moreover, it was theoretically illegal for Spaniards to espouse any religion other than Catholicism.

But the protection enjoyed by the church came to an abrupt end in the 1960s, when Franco lost his paralyzing grip on Spain. The church and the state were officially separated by the Second Vatican Council of 1967; and since then, one internal crisis after another has steadily weakened Spanish Catholic hegemony.

Churchmen Leave the Priesthood

Contradictions between abstract Christian values and the daily reality of supporting a cruel military dictatorship led growing numbers of priests, bishops and other clergymen to leave the church. Since the beginning of the 1970s, more than 2,000 Spanish clerics have left the priesthood. The importance of this exodus, according to Magdalena, lies less in the numbers than in the kinds of men who have left.

"The best are gone," Magdalena says. "Those who were the most educated, most qualified and most conscientious lost heart and interest, because they saw that the church could not transform itself sufficiently. And I suspect there are many more who will be leaving."

For instance, Father José Maria Diez-Alegria, a noted theologian has left. After a painstaking evaluation of Catholic history and liturgy, Diez-Alegria began publicly to charge the Spanish Catholic Church with betraying basic Christian values. When he refused to retract his criticisms, he was politely removed from his Jesuit teaching post.

"You can be sure that if Jesus were alive today," Diez-Alegria says, "it would be the multinational corporations that would kill him, not the Communists. Jesus spoke out against the rich and the powerful and supported equality. I think that if the Catholic Church were true to the teachings of Jesus Christ, it would do the same thing."

Of the 125,000 clerics in Spain, 10 percent to 15 percent manage to outrage the ecclesiastical hierarchy even more by participating in Communist Party activities. One such cleric is Father Agustin Daurda, a 30-year-old Jesuit priest with an active membership in the Central Committee of the Spanish Communist Party in the Catalonia region.

"The church," Daurda says, "lacks credibility. People say, 'If the church deceived us all those years with Franco, why should we think it is not going to do so now?' We progressive Christians have done the church a favor. We've given it a new face, one of democracy and human rights, which it can present proudly to the public. Without us, it (the church) would be left with four old men and a few inept youngsters."

After its appearance this spring, the new Concordat will take a formal step toward separating the power of the church and the state—a process that began under King Juan Carlos several years ago. The king relinquished his power to appoint bishops to a Spanish ecclesiastical council, and the church, in turn, gave up its right to arrest and try those under church orders.

Furthermore, in last June's elections, the Christian Democratic Party—the party most identified with the church—received less than two percent of the vote, making its presence in the new parliament practically nonexistent. Because of this, conservative, money-minded Catholics are particularly worried. They fear that the government can now gather the votes necessary to initiate a national free educational system. The advent of such a system would seriously weaken the state-subsidized private Catholic schools, the church's primary source of revenue.

The Spanish Catholic Church, then, is in serious trouble. For too long it was on the "wrong" side. For too long it divorced itself from the needs of the Spanish people. One suspects that only divine intervention can now save that institution from further decline in modern, secular Spain.

SPANISH REFUGEES: STILL WAITING [6]

King Juan Carlos I of Spain and his government are eager to join the Common Market and end Spain's isolation from Europe. The time has therefore come for Spain to give unconditional restitution to the thousands of Spanish political exiles living all over the world today. These people lost their homes, jobs and country when the fascist rebel generals, supported by Hitler and Mussolini, defeated the legitimate government of Spain after almost three years of war. And, like their most eminent countryman, the late Pablo Casals, they have refused to return until Spain is free of fascism.

Of the 500,000 political refugees who fled to France in 1939 about 40,000 are still living there. Many remain of the 60,000 who went to Mexico and Latin America; 30,000 fled to Africa, but there are only a few there now. There are still some refugees in Australia, Belgium, Canada, England, Sweden, the Soviet Union and the United States. All these people are under the mandate of the United Nations High Commissioner for Refugees.

How have these exiles lived for 36 years? When France opened its borders on January 27, 1939, some 280,000 Republican Army men (including 10,000 wounded), 60,000 male civilians and 170,000 women and children entered.

The French confined many in concentration camps, surrounded by barbed wire and guarded by soldiers with machine guns. The two largest camps were at Argelès-sur-Mer and St. Cyprien on the Mediterranean. Until barracks were put up several months later, these refugees slept on the sand had very little to eat, and their only protection from rain and snow were the blankets they brought with them. It is not surprising that many of those who survived are chronically ill today.

[6] From "Spanish Refugees: Waiting," by Nancy Macdonald, director of Spanish Refugees Aid, Inc. New York *Times.* p 29. Ja. 30, '76. © 1976 by The New York Times Company. Reprinted by permission.

After a few months in France, about 100,000 refugees returned to Spain, many of them forcibly. Many of the Republicans extradited died in Spanish prisons or were shot by firing squads. Those who remained in the camps were eventually used as forced laborers.

When the Nazis took over France, they used these exiles to build the Atlantic Wall and sent 48,000 to Germany for forced work, or to live and die in such concentration camps as Mauthausen and Dachau. Francisco Largo Caballero, Prime Minister of Republican Spain, survived Oranienberg —but 16,000 exiles died in Germany. The postwar West German Federal Government has given restitution to some of their families in Spain and France.

Many escaped from Nazi forced labor in France and joined the Resistance. Anthony Eden has remarked in the House of Commons: "For every five Maquis, three were Spanish Republicans." These exiles also fought with the French Army from Narvik to Tobruk and were among the first to enter liberated Paris.

Ever since World War II the Spanish exiles in France have often lived on the edge of starvation. They were the last hired and first fired, were often not enrolled under social security, and their retirement pensions have been minimal. The skilled and healthy made their way but thousands have lived miserably, waiting for the day when they could return to their country.

The refugees are glad that the "tyrant," the "monster" is dead, but they are waiting to see which way Spain will go. Antonio, who was a pilot in the Republican Air Force and lost both legs when he was shot down by the rebels, says he is waiting for a military amnesty. Flora, who spent 12 years in Generalissimo Francisco Franco's prisons, will never return until a real amnesty is proclaimed. Teresa writes, "We don't have much faith in the new King, who is the spiritual son of the dictator."

The refugees love their country deeply, but the few who have returned usually have gone only to die and be buried in Spanish soil. It is time for these refugees to be taken back with open arms and given full restitution. Then Europe will know that the new Government is serious about its new look and ready to join the twentieth century.

IV. SPAIN'S REGIONAL UNREST

EDITOR'S INTRODUCTION

The drive toward regional autonomy, long repressed by the Franco dictatorship, has arisen again in such regions as the Basque country, Catalonia, Andalusia, and the islands. James M. Markham, a special correspondent of the New York *Times*, first gives a brief survey of this regional unrest in the cities of Málaga and Tenerife.

The region of Catalonia, a nation struggling to be reborn, is discussed by David H. Rosenthal who writes frequently about Catalan culture and politics. The Andalusians in the south and the Basques in the north of Spain are dealt with in two articles by Stanley Meisler, the Los Angeles *Times* correspondent in Madrid. Joe Gandelman, special correspondent of *The Christian Science Monitor*, writes of the Canary Isles, one of Spain's few remaining overseas possessions.

SPANISH REGIONAL UNREST [1]

Spain's political temperature has risen sharply following deadly confrontations between demonstrators and the police in Málaga and the Canary Islands, which are both plagued by heavy unemployment, and with the specter of further trouble in the volatile Basque region.

The violence, which left two youths dead, has underlined the explosive linkage between regional aspirations, economic decline and municipalities and police forces that still act as if the Franco dictatorship were intact.

[1] From "Spaniards Shaken by Regional Unrest," by James M. Markham, Madrid correspondent. New York *Times*. p A7. D. 16, '77. © 1977 by The New York Times Company. Reprinted by permission.

On [December 12, 1977] on Tenerife, the largest of the Canary Islands, the paramilitary Civil Guard shot to death a university student and wounded another after a general strike proclaimed by a small left-wing union turned unruly.

Yesterday, two policemen standing guard outside a Tenerife department store were wounded by shotgun fire; a tiny Algerian-supported movement that seeks independence for the Canaries said it was responsible. Reinforcements of antiriot policemen have been airlifted into the Atlantic islands and the university in Tenerife has been closed until January.

Communist Is Shot to Death

Last week in Málaga, the police reacted more than firmly when in the course of a demonstration in favor of autonomy for Andalusia a group of youths attempted to raise the green-and-white regional flag at city hall. A 19-year-old Communist was shot to death and, after protests were called, scores of people were injured. A Socialist legislator was struck by a policeman as he left the civil governor's office.

"We are sorry about all the deaths," declared General Manuel Prieto López of the Civil Guard yesterday, "but we cannot allow ourselves to be killed without using the means that have been placed in our hands." The general suggested that other, less heavily armed forces should be used in civil disturbances.

For almost a year the Government of Prime Minister Adolfo Suárez has been talking about withdrawing the powerful Civil Guard to rural areas and supplying it with special antiriot control devices that would avoid the loss of life. But in tense situations, notably in the case of Málaga, the police have shown themselves to be outside the control of civilian authority.

Moreover, throughout Spain, mayors and other provincial officials from the Franco era remain in their posts and often show little inclination to keep the police in check.

"There remains intact a provincial world that from positions of responsibility continues to reflect concepts of the past," wrote Lorenzo Contreras, a Madrid columnist. "The absence of a political rupture after Franco has made it possible that two disparate worlds try to coexist under the same roof and inside the same institutions."

The effects of a deepening economic recession are felt unevenly across Spain and in times of trouble give an extra edge to demonstrations in poor regions. Málaga's depressed construction industry, geared to tourist-related building on the Costa del Sol, has laid off thousands and, as a Madrid daily noted today, the Canary Islands have "the highest rate of illiteracy, infantile mortality, emigration, delinquency and unemployment" in Spain.

Some Suspect a Plot

Some conservative voices see the new unrest as a plot. "The Spanish secret services have detected in the last few days the work inside of Spain of foreign agents, inclined to abet a new destabilizing wave of violence," wrote Abel Hernández, a columnist with close ties to the Government.

Mr. Hernández sees the hand of Algeria behind much of what has happened, while the far-right daily *El Alcázar* blames "the K.G.B. and its Spanish henchmen."

Even more worrisome is the unresolved political situation in the northern Basque provinces, which have been the setting for many of the killings in post-Franco Spain. The Suárez Government, fearful of negative reactions in the politically divided province of Navarre, has delayed approval of a provisional autonomy statute for the Basque region that was negotiated by its Minister of Regional Affairs, Manuel Clavero Arévalo.

The legislators who negotiated the statute, including members of Mr. Suárez's Union of the Democratic Center, have threatened to call mass demonstrations and Mr. Clavero Arévalo is said to be considering resigning if the statute is not accepted.

TOWARDS REGIONAL AUTONOMY [2]

A renewal of Spanish political life has to include a restoration of autonomy, human rights, and cultural recognition to those regions of Spain where the people regards itself as a distinct nationality. That is a cumbrous way of putting it, but anything neater would be misleading in one way or another. The whole subject of Spanish regionalism has been sat upon for too long. Spain is not peculiar in that respect. You can say the same of Britain, or France, or Italy. But the history of Iberian regionalism is especially highly charged.

Whenever the lid has come off in the past, different cities and provinces have gone off on their own as if independent, until king or general clamped down and a fresh bout of centralization followed. The new politicians of Madrid know that they have to concede much to the regions, but they also know they have to do it without losing control, or their democratic experiment will not last long. Applying the two principles in practice calls for many delicate decisions.

That you cannot concede human rights in Spain without conceding some regional autonomy is obvious. Suárez has been very free this fall with gestures in that direction, beginning, as he had to, with Catalonia. Obstinately the Catalans persist in celebrating as their *Diada*, their national day, September 11. This is a counter-celebration; on that day in 1714 the first Bourbon king, Philip V, occupied Barcelona after a siege of 13 months, and the Generalidad, the autonomous government of the four provinces of Catalonia, was suppressed.

The *Diada* was celebrated this year with the biggest demonstration Spain has ever seen, an estimated 1.3 million

[2] From article by John Midgley, contributing editor of *The Economist*. *Harper's Magazine*. 256:24-5, 28-9. F. '78. Copyright © 1978 by *Harper's Magazine*. All rights reserved. Reprinted from the February 1978 issue by special permission.

people waving flags and chanting in the streets and squares. Catalonia has six million of Spain's 35 million people, a distinguished culture, and a Latin language rather similar to other languages or dialects of the northwest Mediterranean coast—Provençal, the Languedoc, and Valencian. Unlike many local languages of Europe that have to be kept alive by academics and believers, Catalan seems to have a life of its own, even a magnetism, so that instead of Catalans becoming Castilianized linguistically, as Basques and Galicians tend to be, arrivals in Catalonia tend to be Catalanized in the second generation. Such arrivals are numerous, since Catalonia has been one of the wealthier and busier regions of Spain for the past hundred years. In earlier times it had its ups and downs.

Rich, energetic, and enterprising in the Middle Ages, Catalonia happened to be passing through a prolonged depression, accompanied by a shrinkage of population, at the time the Aragonese and Castilian crowns were united in the persons of Ferdinand and Isabella, the "Catholic monarchs." The routes of economic expansion were shifting from the Mediterranean to the New World, from Catalonia and Aragon, which formed one kingdom, to Castile, the kingdom on the Atlantic which consequently became the dominant component of the future nation-state of Spain. As with other nation-states in Europe, however, an uncertainty remained whether the new nation-state was in reality one nation with several parts, or a conglomeration of several nations.

As late as 1714, when the diplomatists met to put an end to the War of the Spanish Succession, the Portuguese delegates refused to treat with the representatives of Philip V as King of Spain; they said it was the King of Castile they were dealing with. To the Catalans, similarly, Philip might call himself King of Spain but to them he was King of Aragon and consequently Count of Barcelona, because of a medieval marriage that did not affect their national character at all. But Philip was a Frenchman whose grandfather Louis XIV had told him he was going off to Madrid to be King of Spain, and King of Spain, after great bloodshed, he eventually became. He suppressed the political institutions of Catalonia, redrew the administrative divisions, and put the whole kingdom of Aragon, county of Barcelona and all, under the administration of the Council of Castile.

Revival of Catalonia

Catalan institutions remained in a state of suppression until the 1930s, when they were brought briefly to life until crushed again by Franco. This time the government of Catalonia, the Generalidad, avoided total extinction by going into exile for 38 years, returning in the fall of 1977 in the person of its president, a spry old gentleman of 78, Josep Tarradellas, once a counselor to the revered Francesc Marc y Llusa, who had headed the revival of the Thirties.

Sitting at Saint-Martin-le-Beau, in France, Mr. Tarradellas awaited the invitation to return, but when it came he shrewdly insisted that he would return only as president of a revived Generalidad. A majority of the Catalan members of the newly elected Madrid parliament advised King Juan Carlos that this would be the best thing; the king correctly judged that it would be popular in Catalonia; and so it was done. To huge acclamation Mr. Tarradellas was installed as president of Catalonia: but elected by whom, and in charge of what? It had to be done by decree (that is, executive order) from Madrid. Franco's old constitution, still to be replaced by a new one, said nothing about any president of Catalonia. When the new one is ready, a framework will exist within which a Catalan president can be chosen, who will exercise powers, yet to be defined, in concert with a Catalan council and assembly, yet to be elected.

Not much attention has been paid yet to the voices, such as that of the historian and eccentric Socialist politician Josep Benet, that ask what democratic claim Mr. Tarradellas has to preside over Catalonia. The recognition of Mr. Tarradellas as embodiment of the Catalan past is good symbolism, but symbolism is not the same as representative government.

The sum of Mr. Benet's complaints is that by bestowing marks of respect on Mr. Tarradellas the government in

Madrid has won some temporary goodwill, but it has not relaxed its grip on Catalonia, it has not paid its debt or faced the Catalan problem. "For us," says Benet, "Spain is a plurinational state," and there are many Catalans who will concur. How much political weight they can muster has yet to be seen.

With their overseas empires gone and their role as defenders of territory in old-style European wars reduced to the absurd, the European nation-states have lost important sources of authority, just at the time when their power over their financial and economic affairs has been diluted from outside as well, by supranational bureaucracies and multinational corporations. Now long-silent ethnic groups are being emboldened to question not just the merits but the reality of what the grand governments in the great capitals are doing, or can do, in relation to them. So it goes with the Welsh, the Scots, the Bretons, the Corsicans, and the Sicilians. So it goes in Spain.

The Basque Country

The Basque country is the part of Spain most alienated from the Spanish mainstream. Through the centuries Basque villages flourished by keeping non-Basque rulers (Visgoths, Arabs, Frankish emperors, Aragonese, Hapsburgs, Bourbons) at arm's length, maintaining laws and customs of their own, paying tax by treaty instead of by assessment. The Basque towns made a pile in iron and shipping in the nineteenth century; today they are depressed and in grave need of capital for modernization.

The Basqués do not emulate the culture or the style of other Spaniards; they prefer their own. Their language is totally exotic. In Castilian provinces close by, restraint and economy mark speech, gesture, and even facial expression. A Basque crowd is full of noise and movement, it pushes and shoves, and chatters like a migration of starlings. What the Basques have demonstrated for centuries is that they are extremely difficult to govern by anybody but themselves.

Usually in Spain, political enlightenment has been associated with strengthening the central government, homogenizing the laws, and making the national administrative system symmetrical. No such approach works with the Basques. When it is tried, not only does the distant central power get a bloody nose, Basque communal life itself is damaged. General Franco's policy toward his Basque provinces was to keep soldiers and police there from other Spanish regions to maintain order. Treated as an occupied territory, they generated the psychology of an occupied territory. When Basque patriotism was treated as anti-Spanish, it became anti-Spanish.

Like the Catalans, the Basque autonomist leaders who briefly took office under the Republic fled, when Franco entered Bilbao, into exile. Death and dissension, in Mexico, Argentina, the United States, Britain, and France, left a much-changed handful of old gentlemen waiting in the French Basque town of Bayonne 40 years later, with no more than a symbolic and sentimental claim to leadership. In their absence a new breed of Basque leaders had come into existence in their home country, the commandos of the ETA (the initials stand for *Euzkadi ta Azkatasuna,* "Basqueland and Freedom") produced by 40 years of repression. Violent young men who conducted fund-raising bank robberies, harried Franco's "forces of order" with dynamite and gunfire, and still terrorize those who cooperated with authority, they are separatists, not autonomists. They cannot win elections, but they can demand and get protection and concealment from the entire Basque population. No revival of Spanish democracy or triumph of reason in Spanish government holds any interest for them, since they reject Spain itself.

So the underground warfare goes on. Last year's elections produced a body of Basque members of parliament who agreed to recognize the old exiles in Bayonne as the Basque council of government, in the hope that these two groups together could negotiate a statute of autonomy with the government and parliament in Madrid, and bring back peace to the Basque country. What stands in their way i that Basques who want a sensible arrangement with Madrid are liable to be beaten up or gunned down in the streets.

No talk of Catalans or Basques can do justice to the general exuberance of regional impulses and autonomous stirrings, which are felt also in Aragon and Valencia, in Galicia and Andalusia. Since the new constitution will permit regions to be autonomous or not, as they choose, the Suárez government has realized that something has to be done about those regions that have showed perceptible autonomist stirrings but lack a government in exile to negotiate with. So the government has gone out in front in almost every region at once, trying to seize the leadership of autonomism for Madrid. The method is to assemble the congressmen and senators from each region in the region's chief town to consider what to do about autonomy. This should provide the central government with a negotiating partner able to speak for the region and to give weight to the national interest at the same time. Fair enough: but since autonomy is the fashion, and centralism a bad word, the procedure may give birth to rather more autonomy statutes and regional governments than there are ethnic identities, or than people seriously want. In the long run people resent being given more layers of government than are useful.

The Role of Castile

To the extent that the Spanish empire and kingdom had a ruling ethnic group, it was Castilian, so it is well understood that an autonomist movement has to take on something of an anti-Castilian character. The problem is, as the Basque situation most acutely shows, to tame the anti-Castilian rhetoric before it becomes anti-Spanish.

Where does it all leave the Castilians themselves? Theirs is the standard language of Spanish culture. They were dominant in the reconquest of the peninsula, in the exploration of the New World, in the formation of the Spanish nation. The lore, the history books, and the well-rooted prejudices of Catalans and other ethnic minorities cast them in the centralist, exploiting role. Not a bit of it, say writers and economists in the Old Castilian provinces: the central government, oscillating between dreams of empire and appeasement of the outlying Iberian cultures, has always neglected them shamefully. So, last spring, a Castile-León Alliance formed in Valladolid to pursue autonomy for the eleven provinces of León and Old Castile—roughly, north-central Spain from the Guadarrama Mountains (which run north of Madrid) to Santander on the Bay of Biscay.

Madrid as capital of Castile or Spain was a royal invention of a later time. The older cities of southern or New Castile, colonized from Old Castile as the "Reconquest" from the Moors went southward, were just as active in the Comuneros movement as their northern neighbors. They do not feel themselves any less Castilian than Salamanca or Valladolid. A citizen of Toledo, a town of New Castile once the capital of Visigothic *Hispania*, wrote in October to the editor of *Informaciones* in Madrid to declare his indignation at the so-called Castile-León Alliance. His objection to this variation of autonomism was that it left an ancient province like Toledo out in the cold, merely because it belonged to New Castile. "There are few reasons for excluding Toledo from the Castilian community," he wrote, "and none of them historical." He wanted it known that Toledo was just as neglected and ill-governed as the old Castilian provinces. Most of all he resented people drawing regional maps that put Toledo in something called a "central region." This lumped it in with Madrid, and he could not stand Toledo, on top of the other injustices it had suffered, being "degraded to a safety valve for the Madrid megalopolis of the future."

This gentleman of Toledo has a point. Concessions to the peculiarities of ethnically distinct regions are one thing. Imposing a federal principle on the whole country is another. The first is a necessity, without which human rights are hollow. The second is a matter of national political choice, to be done right, or not at all.

With patience, circumspection, and ingenuity, Spain is

being steered from a system of government that overrode people's wishes to a new one designed to pay attention to them. Such an operation (and Suárez, Juan Carlos, and the other political leaders deserve great credit for it) puts a premium on compromise, on making allowances, on knowing when to retreat. There may be moments when leadership will be needed as well, but leadership is something the Spanish people feels it has had more than enough of in the past generation: if mentioned at all, it has to be no more than murmured. Still, when fateful choices are being made, where is the substitute for leadership?

NEW DAY FOR CATALONIA [3]

Basically, Catalonia is defined by its language. Spain has four major languages—Basque, Castilian, Galician, and Catalan, which is a Romance tongue similar to Occitan (a language also sometimes called "provençal" or *langue d'oc*). Catalan is spoken in the provinces of Barcelona, Girona, Lleida, Tarragona, the Balearic Islands, Alacant, Castelló, and Valencia. (Outside of Spain, it is the official tongue of Andorra and is spoken in a small strip of Southern France that includes Perpinyà [Perpignan] and Prades, and in the Sardinian town of l'Alguer.) The historical heartland of the Catalan nation is the "Principality"—that is, the four provinces of Barcelona, Girona, Lleida, and Tarragona. The second major Catalan-speaking area is "the Valencian Land": Alacant, Castelló, and Valencia. The third is the Balearic Islands: Majorca, Minorca, Iviza, and Formentera. Together, these areas form "the Catalan Lands."

This common language is one of the chief expressions of Catalonia's national identity. Some of Europe's most outstanding literature, both in medieval and Renaissance times and during the past century, was written in Catalan. Indeed,

[3] Article by David H. Rosenthal who writes frequently about Catalan culture and is the author of *Modern Catalan Poetry: An Anthology. Inquiry.* 1:13-17. My. 1, '78. Copyright 1978 by Cato Institute, 1700 Montgomery St., San Francisco, CA 94111. Reprinted with permission.

a case could be made for Catalonia as one of the most creative nations in twentieth-century Europe. Though its literature remains largely unknown in the United States, a list of some major Catalan painters, sculptors, and architects should suggest the force of such a claim: Antoni Gaudí, Picasso, Joan Miró, Juli Gonzàlez, Salvador Dalí, Antoni Tàpies, and Joan Ponç. These names in themselves evoke the volatile spirit of modern Catalan culture as a whole: playful but emotionally charged, deeply rooted in the land yet ardently experimental.

Catalan culture, like the language itself, has always been far closer to that of Occitania (a region of southern France) and Northern Italy than to the interior of Spain. In addition, Catalan social structure differs dramatically from that of the rest of the Iberian peninsula. The most powerful single class in the old Catalan-Aragonese kingdom was its energetic mercantile bourgeoisie. Despite periods of weakness, this class has given a special character to subsequent Catalan history. Catalans are known within Spain—sometimes with scorn, sometimes with admiration—as an unusually hard-working people unhampered by aristocratic conventions. (This characteristic is a long-standing one. Statistics from the eighteenth century, for example, show that in the Bishopric of Burgos in Castile a full third of the heads of family were nobility and therefore forbidden to engage in trade or industry; however, in the Principality only one percent of the heads of family were members of the nobility.) Apart from the bourgeoisie, Catalonia has had a prosperous and independent peasantry and a large number of artisans and small traders (called *menestrals*). These two groups—peasants and *menestrals*—are closely linked to each other through the traditional Catalan system of primogeniture, under which the firstborn sons of peasant families would help their younger brothers set themselves up in trade or some craft. The class of *menestrals* has probably contributed more than any other to the special flavor of modern Catalan culture and society. (A new class, the industrial proletariat, has also emerged as an important social force during the past century.)

In Castile, for example, one quickly notices the absence of these energizing groups. Instead one finds other classes—a parasitic aristocracy, landless agricultural laborers, a corrupt and backward clergy—that have never existed in modern Catalonia. The enlightened Catalan middle class and industrial bourgeoisie have no parallel elsewhere in Spain.

All these factors—language, culture, economic structure, and what we might vaguely call a "Mediterranean world view"—have played their part in making Catalonia one of the most highly developed and sharply defined of Europe's stateless nationalities. One particularly telling example is the fact that in 1975, four-fifths of all Spanish women on the birth control pill lived in Catalonia. In terms of "straight politics," the Valencian Land and the Principality both recently delivered clear majorities to the left. Catalan remains the language most commonly heard in the region's major cities. There are hundreds of thousands of Catalan books in print, including scientific texts, car repair manuals, and murder mysteries, along with a large number of translations of authors ranging from Homer to William Faulkner. *Today*, the first Catalan-language daily newspaper since the Civil War, has reached a circulation of 70,000. There are Catalan radio stations and plans for a Catalan television channel. Though on the defensive for 38 of the last 40 years, Catalan, the language, and Catalanism, as a political movement, are anything but moribund.

Catalonia to Gain New Autonomy

How, then, does the situation currently stand? The new Spanish constitution, though still only in draft form, refers to Spain's various nationalities in two articles:

Article 2: The constitution recognizes and the Monarchy guarantees the right of Spain's different nationalities and regions to autonomy.

Article 4: Castilian is the official state language. All Spaniards have the duty to know it and the right to use it.

Spain's other languages will also be official within those nations and regions that accept them as such in their respective autonomous regimes.

Spain recognizes in the richness of the State's various languages a cultural heritage that should be the object of special respect and protection.

All this, of course, is a far cry from Francoism. Nonetheless, the constitution leaves all the concrete details of autonomy open to negotiation. Although the entire matter is still in a highly fluid state, it appears that the Principality will be allowed some powers of taxation, a police force (though precisely how big and of what kind is not known), control over its school system, and some limited legislative powers. In addition, the Spanish Senate will be composed of representatives of Spain's autonomous areas. In other words, all of Spain, including Castile, will have regional governments with greater or lesser powers. As it stands now, autonomy can only be requested by an area's parliamentary delegation. The areas that have requested it so far are Andalusia, Aragón, Valencia, the Basque provinces (which have been negotiating with the central government for the past two months), and Galicia. The Balearics are on the point of requesting autonomy.

Of all these regions and nationalities, the one that has moved most quickly has been the Principality. President Tarradellas recently named seven cabinet ministers, and three of them (the ministers of labor, education, and health) were from the left. Within the Catalan political spectrum, Tarradellas himself falls somewhere between center and right. For this reason, Prime Minister Suárez chose to negotiate with Tarradellas's representatives as well as with the Catalan parliamentary delegation. The parliamentarians acquiesced because Tarradellas was the only single figure who could authoritatively speak for Catalonia. Old and in rather poor health, he can hardly continue for long as President. Nor is he genuinely well liked in Catalan political circles. His conservative political positions and his high-handed manner with his colleagues have alienated many of his influential countrymen. For example, Tarradellas recently expelled Josep Benet, a distinguished historian and member of the Spanish Senate, from the meetings of the Catalan parliamentarians. Benet was readmitted shortly thereafter, but the incident is typical of Tarradellas's style as a leader.

What Suárez most hoped to avoid, through his discussions with Tarradellas, was the immediate formation of a leftist Catalan government. Nonetheless, it seems almost certain that such a government will exist within a year or two, both in the Principality and in Valencia. In the municipal elections scheduled for next spring, it appears that the Socialists and Communists will emerge with a clear combined majority in most Catalan cities. A similar result is expected when elections are held for the *Generalitat*'s legislature. This projected left government is also one primary reason for the strength of Catalanism among "immigrants" who—apart from their desire for cultural integration—realize that Catalanism offers them the best immediate chance to live under socialism.

A Resurgence of Anarchism

A final factor worth mentioning here is the recent resurgence of anarchism. During Franco's reign the anarchist trade union federation (the CNT) virtually disappeared. The illegal Workers' Commissions that sprang up during the 1960s and early 1970s were largely dominated by the Communists. In the last two years, however, the anarchists have made up for lost time. Their strength in the Catalan labor movement has grown from almost nothing to a position approximately equal to that of the Communists. One cause of this growth was the Communist Party's discouragement of strikes during the parliamentary election campaign. Many workers struck anyway, and found themselves obliged to call on the CNT for help. In addition to the proletariat, another major nucleus of anarchism in Catalonia is found among students and the young in general. Though anarchists refuse to participate in electoral politics, it is possible that they will come to function as a kind of pressure group. Since they view communism as an immediately realizable goal, they can be expected to push any leftist government to take serious steps in that direction.

At this point, however, one can make no definite predictions. The problem of Catalans today—as during the 1930s—is that they are out of step with the conservative areas of Spain. Most Catalans feel they must move cautiously in order to consolidate their recent gains. For the time being, therefore, more "extreme" Catalanist groups like the PSAN (Socialist Party of National Liberation) have only limited support. What the PSAN advocates is the total independence and union of all the Catalan lands. It believes that Catalonia can never realize itself within a more conservative and backward Spain. If events prove the PSAN right, the independence movement can be expected to grow. For the moment, however, most Catalans are willing to wait and see what happens. Barring a rightist coup, Spain will certainly move towards an increasingly decentralized regime. Indeed, it must do so, for nowhere in Europe is attachment to the state so weak as in Spain. What many Catalans hope to see eventually is the inclusion of Spain within a United States of Europe composed of national units like Catalonia, Brittany, and Scotland, rather than centralized states. In the meantime they hope that their nation will again become—as it was during the 1930s—a model of progressive and imaginative government both for the Mediterranean area and for Western Europe as a whole.

ANDALUSIAN UNREST [4]

This [Lebrija, Spain] is the heart of Andalusia, where the houses glisten with whitewash, the women wear black and the men, for much of the year, do not work.

[4] From "Andalusian Unemployment Stirs Unrest," by Stanley Meisler, correspondent in Madrid. Los Angeles *Times*. p 1 IV & 4 IV. Ap. 16, '78. Copyright 1978. Los Angeles Times. Los Angeles Times/Washington Post News Service. Reprinted with permission.

Angry, truculent while replying to questions, 56-year-old Juan Cordero Fuente did have some work on a recent morning here in Lebrija. He was part of a gang of 30 farm laborers who, for 738 pesetas ($9.23) a day each, were digging a ditch in a street that probably does not need to be dug. They are taking part in a program of "community works" that the Spanish government has set up to avoid an explosion of desperation in depressed Andalusia.

Cordero was dressed in what amounts to the uniform of the *jornalero* (day laborer) of the Andalusian farm belt: a cap, jacket, sweater and baggy trousers.

In staccato sentences, he told his story. He last had farm work in December, picking cotton. He and his nine children, ranging in age from 8 to 26 years, earned a total of 2,000 pesetas ($25) a day in cotton. Since the new year, he has had 15 days of "community works" and nothing else.

Cordero is one of 100,000 jornaleros who are classified as unemployed, a quarter of the total agricultural work force in Andalusia. But the classifications of employed and unemployed have little meaning here. At the most, a day laborer can hope to find four months of farm work a year in Andalusia now. His situation is desperate, whether he is employed or unemployed.

The problem is so hopeless that the Spanish Labor Party, a radical party to the left of the Communists, has its only strength in Spain here in Andalusia. Many day laborers belong to the Spanish Labor Party's farm union, the Syndicate of Farm Workers (known from its initials in Spanish as SOC). At the end of February, SOC led 5,000 unemployed jornaleros in a symbolic occupation of plantations. The publicity galvanized the Spanish government into speeding up its appropriation of funds for "community works" and its distribution of plots of idle land to the unemployed.

The plight of the day laborers has nourished radical movements and outbursts of violence in Andalusia for almost 200 years, and the government obviously is trying to head off any renewal of trouble.

In his office in Seville 45 miles north of Lebrija, Luis

Fernández Madrid, the governor of Seville province, said recently, "It is a situation of potential danger. Hunger is a bad counselor. When men are hungry and out of work, it is like gunpowder. In some way, if someone lights a match, it could explode."

Andalusia: Spain's Most Depressed Area

Andalusia, comprising the eight most southern provinces of Spain, is the most depressed area of a country caught in severe economic crisis. The five provinces with the highest percentage of unemployment in Spain are all Andalusian. With a population of 6.2 million, one-sixth of Spain's total population, Andalusia has a rate of unemployment among all workers of 18 percent.

Andalusia has been in perpetual depression since the Catholic kings of Spain conquered it and took it away from the Arabs in the thirteenth, fourteenth, and fifteenth centuries. The kings rewarded nobles from Castile with huge tracts of Andalusian land. The landlords worked these plantations with Arab slaves and with poor Spanish farmers pushed off their own land. The unemployed jornaleros of today are descended from those slaves and poor Spaniards.

In the nineteenth century, the government created more large estates by selling church and common lands to the highest bidders. As a result, more than half the agricultural land of Andalusia now is concentrated among fewer than two percent of the farms. Andalusia has a fifth of all Spanish farms larger than 500 acres.

Most historians blame the large landowners, known contemptuously in Andalusia as *senoritos*, for standing in the way both of land reform and of industrialization of the region. Profits from the plantations of olive trees and cotton have been invested elsewhere in Spain. This neglect, according to Andalusian journalist Antonio Burgos, has turned Andalusia into "the Third World, the Latin America of Spain."

Descriptions from the past often sound like descriptions of today. In 1780, for example, the Count of Campomanes, a government minister, wrote, "In Andalusia the inhabitants are nearly all simple laborers who have only temporary and precarious occupation and live the rest of the year in poverty, plunged in inaction, for lack of remunerative work."

British historian Gerald Brenan has estimated that day laborers worked an average of six months a year in the 1930s. For decades, travelers have accused the Andalusians of laziness, citing the way the plazas of the whitewashed towns always seem to fill up during the day with idle men. The plaza of Lebrija fills up the same way now on any sunny day that its 1,000 jornaleros have no work.

The 100,000 jornaleros of Andalusia who do not have enough work now are the miserable remnants of this past. A number of factors have converged this year to make their plight more acute or, at least, more evident.

The Fruits of Farm Mechanization

With costs rising and farm prices held steady by a government more worried about city consumers than rural workers, landowners in Andalusia are mechanizing their farms. Jose Luis de Pablo Romero, whose 6,500-acre plantation was mechanized years ago, said recently, "To compete with Europe, we have to produce the maximum, and we have to do so with maximum mechanization." Other landowners are following his lead.

For the jornalero, there is now the sickening sight throughout Seville province of fallen olive trees, cut down to make way for open wheat fields. Olive trees were picked by hand. Wheat is harvested by machine. The difference can be crushing for a day laborer.

On top of this, some safety valves have clogged. In the last decade, a farm laborer could get some work in the tourist industry on Andalusia's Costa del Sol during the summer or in the construction industry powered by the tourist boom. But tourism is in decline these days, and construction in Andalusia has practically come to a halt.

Perhaps more important, emigration, the major escape route, is closed. Beginning in the 1950s, the Spanish government encouraged industrialization of the northern cities while neglecting Andalusian agriculture. The cheap labor for this industrialization, especially in Barcelona, came from Andalusia. That was part of the government's plan. A day laborer could give up Andalusia and its poverty for a factory job in the north. Or he could answer the call in the rest of Europe for cheap labor. In the 1960s, 959,896 Andalusians emigrated.

But there is no need for cheap Andalusian labor now. Europe is in an economic recession, and Spain is worse off than most other countries. A million Spaniards are out of work, and Barcelona has no jobs now for emigrating Andalusians. In fact, some unemployed Andalusians have returned home from the industrial north. Other jornaleros have discovered that there is not even a need for them as temporary farm laborers in Europe.

A jornalero took an American journalist aside in Lebrija the other day. "I used to go to France every year for a month to pick beets," the jornalero said. "But there wasn't any work in France last year. You're a foreigner. Do you know if there will be any work in France this year?"

It is easy to see why these farm workers are attracted to a political party and a union that promises radical solutions. The Communist and Socialist labor unions have the largest agricultural labor following in Andalusia as a whole. But SOC, which sneers at the Communists as a bourgeois party, dominates labor in those towns like Lebrija that have large concentrations of unemployed jornaleros.

In February, Francisco Caseros, the 29-year-old secretary of SOC, refused to join the Communists and Socialists in sponsoring a massive but restrained demonstration against unemployment. Instead, a week later he led 5,000 jornaleros in an occupation of three government plantations and two private plantations for several hours. His action obviously upset the government of King Juan Carlos and Premier Adolfo Suárez.

The occupation was symbolic. "They occupied the plantations by putting sticks into the ground," Governor Fernandez Madrid said, "as if they were Columbus discovering America or Balboa discovering the Pacific in the name of Isabella, the Catholic queen."

There is no doubt that this is true. But Caseros is an excitable young man, angry about the problems of Andalusia, quick to make rash statements. Wearing a parka in his office in Seville, he recently addressed two American journalists as if they were a large meeting of jornaleros. "Yesterday it was symbolic," he said of SOC's occupation of land. "Tomorrow it will not be symbolic."

The Role of Anarchism

Caseros and other SOC leaders like to make references to the anarchist past of Andalusia and to the historical uprising of Casas Viejas in 1933. In that incident, desperate farm workers, led by an anarchist, besieged the headquarters of the hated *Guardia Civil*, Spain's paramilitary rural police, and maintained the siege until army troops came into the town and suppressed the peasant uprising with great bloodshed. SOC leaders are obviously warning that history could repeat itself if the problems of Andalusia are allowed to fester.

Until the Spanish Civil War, the anarchist labor union had an almost mystical mass following among poor rural workers in Andalusia. This is no longer true. But, in the view of journalist Burgos, "SOC is occupying the ground once held in Andalusia by the Anarchist." That is what troubles the government.

The government reacted swiftly to the publicity over SOC's symbolic occupation of land. It already had announced increased appropriations of funds for "community works" in Andalusia and its intention of distributing some government land to jornaleros. But Spanish government announcements often promise more than is delivered. In this case, the government seems to have followed through.

For the province of Seville alone, the government appropriated almost $19 million for "community works" in the first quarter of 1978. Another $10 million was made available for government projects in the province. Two weeks after the symbolic occupation of land, every one of the thousand jornaleros classified as unemployed in Lebrija had work, either in nearby beet fields or in "community works." If all the money allotted does filter to the jornaleros, each one in Seville will have a bit more than $1,000 of work. That would be an adequate substitute for the social security that does not cover jornaleros in Spain.

Redistribution of Land

By mid-March, the government of Seville province, through lottery, had picked 1,100 jornaleros to receive 30-acre tracts of land, 405 going to the workers of Lebrija. This fulfilled part of the demand of SOC that land should belong to those who work it. But it was not likely to alleviate much of the problem.

Land is of little use to jornaleros who have no capital, credit or machinery and have never had the experience of managing a farm. Caseros and other SOC officials are urging the lottery winners to pool their land into some kind of a cooperative. But this may be a difficult concept to the individualistic Andalusian.

Surrounded by SOC officials shouting that a cooperative could do better than one man, 35-year-old Jose Pena Carrasco, the winner of a tract of land in Lebrija, pointed to his fellow workers in "community works" and said, "we are supposed to be working together and we can't even dig one yard of ditch a day."

Although there is disagreement about the worth of such stopgap measures as the distribution of land, there is a good deal of agreement among Andalusian landowners, Socialists, Communists and SOC officials about what needs to be done for Andalusian agriculture in the long run.

Whether senorito or SOC, an Andalusian will say that the government must end its policy of neglecting agriculture, must raise farm prices through a subsidy system, and must encourage investment for the development of agricultural industries like canning or processing.

Under the Arabs and the Romans before them, Andalusia was a great agricultural area. Many experts insist it still has that potential. "Andalusia is not poor," said Francisco Caseros. "But when you live in Andalusia, you are poor."

SPAIN'S ABUSED BASQUES [5]

There is a stubborn bitterness within the Basque people that the rest of Spain refuses to understand and accept, and this combination of feelings endangers order and democracy in Spain.

The recent celebration of Basque National Day and the recriminations that followed illustrate the problem. Cool heads did not prevail and the intractable, deeply rooted Basque problem cries out for coolness and patience.

The Basques dominate an industrialized nub of land in northern Spain that has a population of 2.5 million. Out of revenge for their spirited resistance during the civil war and out of his obsession with the idea of a powerful, centralized Spanish state, the late dictator Gen. Francisco Franco tried to wipe out Basque culture. To an extent, he succeeded. Few Basques now speak their ancient language well. But this has only intensified their resentment and alienation.

For 41 years, the Basques were not permitted to celebrate Aberri Eguna—the Basque National Day—on Easter Sunday. But the Basque provinces, like several other regions, have been given what the central government calls "preautonomy," and a celebration of Aberri Eguna was authorized by Madrid this year.

More than 200,000 Basques marched in Bilbao, San Sebastián, Vitoria and Pamplona. It was a day of peaceful demonstrations, without the bloody confrontations between police and Basques that have marred so many illegal street

[5] From "Spain's Abused Basques Are Bitter," by Stanley Meisler, correspondent in Madrid. Los Angeles *Times*. p 6 V. Ap. 9, '78. Copyright 1978. Los Angeles Times. Los Angeles Times/Washington Post News Service. Reprinted with permission.

rallies of the past. Basque leaders were pleased with the day's observance.

But Spaniards in Madrid found disturbing signs: The main banner in the Bilbao march called not for "autonomy" but for "self-determination." Extremists in the crowds shouted their support of independence and of the Basque guerrilla organization *Euzkadi ta Azcatasuna* (ETA). The marchers carried Basque flags but no Spanish flags. In Bilbao, marchers tore down a Spanish flag from a building and burned it.

Madrid reacted as if the Spanish state were under siege. Newspapers in the capital condemned the separatists. Lt. Gen. Manuel Gutierrez Mellado, the vice premier and minister of defense, made a well-publicized speech to paratroopers in which he proclaimed that "Spain is one, and we are not going to let anyone break it." The Committee of Defense of the Spanish Parliament swiftly pledged its support of the general's patriotic sentiments.

It is obvious that some Basques went too far in their zeal for celebrating Aberri Eguna. But Spanish officialdom went just as far in its overreaction. Neither attitude made the Basque problem any easier.

The government of King Juan Carlos and Premier Adolfo Suárez decreed pre-autonomy for the Basques at the end of last year. Pre-autonomy is a device for placating chauvinist feelings while the Cortes—the Spanish parliament —writes a constitution that will allow some regional autonomy.

Under pre-autonomy, the Basques have a Basque general council and a president, Socialist Ramon Rubial. But this "government" has no powers. The members of the council have even paid the Basque government's expenses out of their own pockets while waiting for an appropriation from Madrid. Pre-autonomy is a shell without much inside.

Yet pre-autonomy is an emotional safety valve. If they did not already have it, the Basques would be demonstrating in the streets for it. But besides its psychological sop, pre-autonomy has allowed a regional government to be set up to negotiate regional powers for itself once the constitution is approved. But, the Basques may be disappointed not only in the evolving constitution, but in their ability to shape an acceptable autonomy. During the 1930s, the Basques had autonomy that gave them fewer powers than an American state. Although they declared themselves a republic for a short while during the civil war, they were able to do so only because they were separated from Madrid by Franco's armies. The present Spanish government does not intend to give them more independence than they had as an autonomous region in the early 1930s.

What Will Follow "Pre-Autonomy"?

The first draft of the constitution, now being revised, hints at what is in store. Although supplementary regional law officers would be allowed, the central government's police would have the main responsibility for maintaining law and order. For years, the Basques have complained that the Madrid-directed police, especially the Guardia Civil, made them feel like an oppressed people under occupation by foreign troops. The constitution, at least in its first draft, would hardly end this grievance.

In addition, the first draft is vague about control of education. It appears to leave that as a matter for negotiation between the regional government and the central government.

The Basques, so bitter about the Franco attempt to wipe out their culture, would feel defrauded by autonomy if it did not allow them to impose an educational curriculum infused with Basque culture and the Basque language.

Disappointment could encourage more violence. Since Franco died on November 20, 1975, there have been 59 political killings in the Basque provinces, more than half the total of political deaths in Spain. The terrorists of ETA have accounted for at least 25 of the deaths.

Some Spaniards thought that these assassinations might end after Spain held its first free parliamentary elections in 41 years last June. But instead, ETA has increased its pace of violence.

ETA, which takes its name from the Basque initials for the slogan, "Basque homeland and freedom," wants to create an independent, Marxist Basque state, uniting the northern Basque provinces of Spain with the southern Basque provinces of France. That position was repudiated by an overwhelming majority of the Basques last June. The Socialist Workers Party and the Basque National Party, two parties that advocate autonomy, not independence, swept the elections.

Nevertheless, ETA has attracted a good deal of sympathy as the chief symbol of resistance to Franco during the years of the dictatorship. As ETA continues to kill, the sympathy is waning. But ETA still has enough support to trouble other Basque leaders.

During Holy Week, the Roman Catholic bishops of Bilbao said, in a pastoral letter condemning ETA violence: "There is no lack of those, taking part in a climate of revenge, who look on such conduct with sympathy. Some even approve of the killings, if they do not demand them irresponsibly with their shouts."

ETA feeds on such sympathy and will probably not stop killing until it feels isolated and demoralized. But the Basques will not isolate ETA until they feel confident of their autonomy.

The Basques thus create a thorny and dangerous problem for Spain. While Spanish officials do not like to admit this, their great fear is that a breakdown of law and order in the Basque provinces might tempt the army to step in and restore law and order. The dangers for democracy in that kind of military initiative are obvious.

The granting of pre-autonomy was an important first step for the Basque region. But a good deal of hard bargaining and realistic analysis must follow. This will be difficult to achieve in the emotional atmosphere of fierce Basque bitterness in the north and volatile Spanish nationalism in Madrid.

SPAIN'S TROUBLED ISLES [6]

At first glance it is all so simple—or so the travel brochures suggest.

Tourists stroll along the boardwalk at Las Canteras Beach. Deep blue waters are set against a background of gray-brown mountains etched from volcanic upheavals ages ago. Shiny new hotels pierce the skyline. There are hundreds of duty-free shops; there are restaurants and cabarets. Jasmine, carnations, and wisteria perfume the air.

But casual tourists do not realize that, as one longtime American resident here puts it, "expenses have doubled. Retirees are thinking about going back to the US" because inflation, plus a 25 percent devaluation of the currency in July, has sent the price of food soaring.

Nor do the tourists realize that the 17 percent unemployment rate here is double Spain's, that scarce water costs $7 to $17 an hour, even though it is often of poor quality, that the already struggling common man's livelihood, fishing, is gravely threatened by recent concessions made by the parent Spanish Government to the African countries of Morocco and Mauritania. (The Canaries are only 80 miles from the African coast, whereas they are 800 miles from Spain.)

Yet, tourists soon sense the artificiality: These seven islands are not as breathtaking as travel literature claims. Parts are dry, barren, and poverty-stricken.

And then there is the radio voice, beamed from Algeria, that also influences the outsider's image of the Canaries.

"Put a percentage of gasoline and a little bit of sugar in a bottle, preferably of dark color," says the cultured but spooky voice. "Don't forget the sugar. Your Molotov cocktail is ready. Canarian, get your Godo."

The voice is that of Antonio Cubillo, an exiled labor lawyer who has waged a 15-year "war" against the "Godos"

[6] Article by Joe Gandelman, special correspondent. *Christian Science Monitor.*) 20. N. 22, '77. Reprinted by permission from *The Christian Science Monitor.* © 1977 The Christian Science Publishing Society. All rights reserved.

(Goths), the Canarians' unflattering term for Spaniards. He fled the islands in 1961 while on provisional liberty following arrest for leading a "non-peaceful" demonstration. A year later he settled in Algeria.

There, he taught at a university and organized the Movement for Self-determination and Independence of the Canaries Archipelago, an "African liberation movement." He asked Algeria for air time seven years ago, but only when the government in Madrid ceded its phosphate-rich colony of Spanish Sahara to rival Morocco and Mauritania in 1975 did the Algerians agree. Thus did the "voice of the free Canaries" debut on Algerian radio.

His proclaimed goal: an independent "socialist" (Marxist) country. His argument: that the islands are culturally distinct from "the peninsula" (Spain).

The Apparent Strategy

His strategy appears to be threefold: (1) Explode bombs. These are then reported in the Spanish press and abroad. (2) Be readily accessible for telephone interviews with foreign correspondents who are attracted by the situation here but think it is worth only a few days of their time, a few interviews, and a bit of description. (3) Point to the resulting —but usually overblown—foreign press reports as "proof" that a popularly supported independence movement exists.

(In fact, Mr. Cubillo's movement may have won as much publicity from two recent bombs that did not explode on schedule as from any that did. Last month police here found the two devices near a spot where King Juan Carlos of Spain was to give a speech and removed them, exploding them later in an empty field. The story was circulated internationally, although Mr. Cubillo claimed the bombs were planted not so much to explode as to draw attention to his cause.)

"He is an anarchist," claims a high government official, "the kind that exists everywhere—and in the US kills presidents."

Nonetheless, demonstrations called against him have flopped, and a local journalist asserts, "When Mr. Cubillo begins talking about capitalism he strikes a responsive chord due to the heavy presence of German businessmen here."

Foreign-Owned Businesses

In 1972, for instance, 61 percent of the tourist and real estate businesses here were foreign-controlled. The biggest investors are Germans, who also make up 26 percent of the tourist trade. The most popular island among Germans is Fuerteventura, one zone of which the local people call "La Pared" (the wall) since Canarians reportedly may not enter.

High government officials insist foreign investment is "good for the country." But many Canarians are unsure. They note that present laws effectively prevent disclosure of who owns what until around 1980. Originally Germans invested in the Canaries due to the tax laws in their own country, which allowed deductions on money invested in developing nations—a policy former Prime Minister Willy Brandt's government finally halted.

Anti-foreign sentiments have been exploited by the separatist extreme Left. But some here suggest Mr. Cubillo has made a positive contribution toward the Canarian outlook.

"He has created a mentality—to question," says Jeronimo Saavedra, one of three moderate leftist Socialist Workers Party (PSOE) parliamentary representatives from the Canaries. "People waited for so many years for problems to be solved. In his broadcasts he raised doubts. His handicap is his distance."

Despite the broadcasts, Canarians on all levels increasingly disown Mr. Cubillo and his approach. But, their voices, unlike his, seldom reach the outside world. Thus, the image persists that Mr. Cubillo's "liberation movement" enjoys the vicarious support of Canarians.

"A movement like Cubillo's would be very difficult here," argues Mr. Saavedra. "Not more than one person here has been wounded in bombings, and there have been no major assassinations. There is no political sensitivity like in the Basque country. People here do not think of demonstrations like people in Bilbao, where 20,000 persons poured out into the streets. People here fear that to demonstrate is to be 'independentista' [a supporter of independence]."

The restraining factor appears to be the Canarian character, which Canarians themselves say is "banana-ized" by the hot climate. The Canarian, with his Latin-American accent, is humble, peaceful, and, some say, apathetic. This enormously frustrates the radicals.

"The Canarian feels he is inferior and unable to protagonize his own historical process," complains Carlos Suárez, a prominent separatist political leader. "The climate and philosophy make us adaptable to human misery. Why do the Canaries continue being part of Spain when Cuba and the Philippines broke away? It is the character of our bourgeoisie. They do not revolt. They are used to living in the shade of Spain."

Election Shocks Left

That shade looms larger since the elections to the Spanish Parliament last June. The elections, which shocked Canarian leftists and delighted Madrid, gave Prime Minister Adolfo Suárez Gonzáles's moderate Democratic Center Party (UCD) 70 percent of the vote here in Las Palmas Province, while the PSOE won 14 percent and Mr. Suárez's United Canary People's Party only six percent. To Carlos Suárez it was a particularly bitter defeat.

The UCD won "a vote of fear, ignorance, and perhaps computers," he scoffs. "For seven years you live in clandestinity. The people hide you. Then, suddenly, they vote for the people who pursued you." He shakes his head: "They voted for my pursuers, not me."

Other moderate leftists assert the UCD vote was largely a reaction to Mr. Cubillo's violent separatism, which had harmed the cause of the more peaceful separatists. Thus, the theory goes, even unemployed workers opted for the UCD as the safest option.

Now, Mr. Cubillo not only finds himself isolated from the far Left here on the islands but also on the Spanish mainland—and that includes the Communist Party and the PSOE. Even the Algerian-backed Polisario Front, which battles Morocco and Mauritania in the Western Sahara, refuses to recognize Mr. Cubillo's movement.

Generally, however, Mr. Cubillo's greatest strength does come from abroad. Since 1968 he has inched closer toward his goal of "Africanizing" the Canaries question. In that year the Organization of African Unity (OAU) agreed the Canaries were "unliberated" African territory held by "colonial" Spain. Still, the OAU has refrained from giving him complete recognition or armed support.

Last July Mr. Cubillo tried again when the OAU met in Libreville, Gabon. Its "liberation committee" finally decided to send an investigatory team to the Canaries to determine whether the islands were "African."

The Madrid government responded by announcing its "profound displeasure" and launched a massive diplomatic blitz to inform OAU countries that the Canaries were non-negotiable and Spanish—and that any investigatory commission would be unwelcome interference in its internal affairs.

Madrid does not see Mr. Cubillo as the chief trouble: "The problem is not Cubillo, but Algeria," complains one Spanish analyst. "It is tearing up OAU meetings with misinformation about the Canaries. Most of these countries have no real idea of what the Canaries are."

Close observers of the situation think Algeria is using Mr. Cubillo as a bargaining chip and would withdraw its support of him if Spain were to tilt its way on the Sahara question.

In the end, the OAU shoved the matter upstairs, to a committee, which merely postpones a decision. Meanwhile, government officials here staunchly maintain that "Canarians are more Spanish than those of us from the peninsula."

Yet, Canarians feel different from and often resentful toward the "peninsula." What they seek is economic and political control over their own region rather than independence. Given time, the conventional wisdom goes, they likely will get such control via an autonomy statute.

V. THE NEW PORTUGAL

EDITOR'S INTRODUCTION

Since the peaceful military coup d'état of 1974 that ended a half century of dictatorship, Portugal has moved toward democracy, but is hampered by an economy so seriously troubled that political repercussions, such as the recent dismissal of Mário Soares and appointment of Alfredo Nobre da Costa as prime minister, are difficult to predict. It is Portugal's related political and economic scenes with which this section mainly deals.

First George W. Grayson, lecturer at the National War College and the Foreign Service Institute of the Department of State, reviews Portugal's new politics. Then Kenneth Maxwell, an associate professor of history at Columbia University and author of the forthcoming *Revolution in Portugal and Angola,* assesses both the negative and positive aspects of Portugal's new democratic experiment.

In the next articles Helen Gibson, special correspondent of *The Christian Science Monitor,* discusses both Portugal's recent swing to the Right politically and its failing economy. The next three articles deal with specific aspects of the nation's economic woes: inflation, worker-run business firms, and a balance of payments deficits. The article on the Catholic church's unease over new civil laws is again by Ms. Gibson. A look at Portugal's active press is taken by Milton Hollstein, professor of communication, University of Utah, Salt Lake City.

PORTUGAL'S NEW POLITICS [1]

On April 25, 1974, Portugal's 48-year-old dictatorship collapsed when young officers of the Armed Forces Movement deposed Prime Minister Marcello Caetano and Presi-

[1] From "Portugal's Crisis," by George W. Grayson, professor of government, College of William and Mary and lecturer at the National War College and the Foreign Service Institute of the Department of State. *Current History.* 73:169-73+. N. '77. Copyright © 1977, by Current History, Inc. Reprinted with permission.

dent Américo Tomás. In the wake of the overthrow, a carnival-like atmosphere enveloped Lisbon: citizens frolicked in the streets with beret-wearing soldiers; students sped through the capital in commandeered police cars; and red carnations appeared everywhere to become the symbol of the "Revolution of Flowers."

The celebrations have long since ceased. Crowds in the street are now likely to be shoppers queuing up for scarce items. After more than two years of haphazard military rule, a new constitutional structure has been erected, complete with a President, A Prime Minister, and a National Assembly. But the hand of the *ancien régime* lies heavy upon this Iberian nation; the new government still struggles to modernize an archaic economy whose residual strength is sapped by revolutionary excesses, sharply higher energy costs and the international recession.

Mário Soares, the Socialist leader who serves as Portugal's Prime Minister, often describes the aims of the 1974 coup as the three "D's"—decolonize, democratize and develop. The first aim was accomplished with the granting of independence to the African nations of Guinea-Bissau (September 1974), Mozambique (June 1975) and Angola (November 1975). The second aim was achieved through the popular selection of a constituent assembly, the drafting of a new fundamental law, and the election of a National Assembly, a President, and municipal officials. The third "D," however, has eluded Soares's government; on the contrary, economic conditions are harsh and bankruptcy has been avoided only by massive infusions of foreign assistance.

Portugal's Economic Malaise

Indicators of economic malaise are ubiquitous. The country's inflation rate, the highest in the Western world, was 26.8 percent in 1976, and is expected to surpass 35 percent in 1977. Unemployment afflicts approximately 17 percent of the nation's 3.2 million active labor force, and underemployment is extremely high in tourism, government service, and the agriculture that employs one-third of the country's workers. The trade deficit in 1976 reached $1.5

billion, a record level, as Portugal purchased twice as much foodstuff as she sold. These conditions have inspired graffiti on walls and buildings throughout Lisbon, which say: "Starvation is just around the corner." Those who have retained a sense of humor under difficult circumstances ask the difference between an optimist and a pessimist. An optimist, so the story goes, believes that all Portuguese will soon be eating horse droppings, while a pessimist insists there will not be enough to go around.

Politicians prefer to whet appetites with promises of an improved tomorrow rather than demanding abstinence and sacrifice today. Soares is no exception. During his first few months in office, he resisted needed austerity measures. Then, on September 9, 1976, prodded by President Antônio Ramalho Eanes, who was increasingly alarmed at the economy's continued stagnation, the 53-year-old bibliophile announced a series of reforms. Designed to improve the country's balance of payments, the program imposed a modest (20-30 percent) surcharge on general consumer imports and a major levy (60 percent) on imported luxuries, required a deposit equal to 50 percent of the value of luxury items, allowed the government to fix quotas on non-essential imports, and created a national council to supervise prices and incomes.

Six months later, as conditions continued to worsen, additional steps were taken. To stimulate exports, attract tourists and encourage investment in Portugal by emigrants, the escudo was devalued 15 percent ($1.00 = 38 escudos). The government also restricted wage increases to 15 percent, offered tax incentives to firms selling goods and services abroad, and imposed price controls on a "shopping basket" of fuels and foodstuffs. Moreover, it boosted the rediscount rate from 6.5 to 8 percent, the sales tax on ordinary goods to 12 percent, and the levy on luxuries to 50 percent. The package included provisions to encourage private savings.

Thus far it is difficult to determine the effect of the reforms, in part because a flood of imports entered the country before the last measures were taken. It is evident, however, that the inflation rate will not fall as Soares had hoped. This will make it difficult for him to continue to restrict wage increases as part of a tripartite social contract among the government, organized labor and employers. Still, the indefatigable Prime Minister has continued to preach the message that only through a wage ceiling can the nation avoid the spiral of devaluation, price increases, wage hikes, more inflation and further devaluation. Even the regime's most ardent supporters, those who take heart from the increased tourism and the upswing in remittances from Portuguese living abroad in 1977, believe that the current austerity measures must be deepened before economic conditions improve.

Starting the New Government

The 1974 coup d'état brought kaleidoscopic changes in the politics of a nation that had been gripped by a dictatorship for nearly a half a century. No fewer than six provisional military-dominated governments attempted to run the country before the June 1976 election in which Eanes captured 61.5 percent of the ballots to become Portugal's first democratically elected President in modern memory.

Exuberant support from Portugal's three major political parties—the Socialists (PS), the moderate Social Democrats (PSD), and the right-leaning Democratic Center Party (CDS) —contributed to Eanes's impressive victory, as did the backing of a broad segment of the military. But the stern, aloof army chief of staff subsequently developed a broad popular following with his pledge to promote social democracy, defend the new constitution, quell insurrection activity and preserve law and order.

Immediately on his inauguration on July 23, the day on which he assumed the additional post of armed forces chief of staff, Eanes named Soares Prime Minister. Since then, the two men have worked closely together: Eanes benefits from Soares's three decades of political experience, while the popular Prime Minister is aided by the President's good judgment and thorough knowledge of the Portuguese military.

Soares has invited into the Cabinet only members of his own Socialist party, military officers, and technocrats. Although the Socialists hold a minority of seats (107) in the 265-member Parliament, the Prime Minister has rejected suggestions that the Social Democrats (73), the CDS (42), or the Communists (40) be enlisted in a coalition government. Instead, he has pursued a strategy of shifting coalitions, seeking support from different parties on each piece of legislation. Such an approach sometimes produces strange bedfellows; for example, changes in the agrarian reform law were passed in mid-1977 over the opposition of the CDS and the Communists (PCP), thanks to the backing of the Social Democrats.

As a moderate, Soares must constantly fend off attacks from the Right, which charges his government with having "fallen asleep" when it comes to combating crime and inflation, and the Left, which accuses him of pursuing a "policy of capitalist, landowner and imperialist recovery." In addition, opposition to the perceived slowness of the pace of reform has erupted within his own Socialist party. In the summer of 1977, the Social Democrats and the CDS, which together boast eight seats more than the Socialists, publicly voiced displeasure at Soares's use of them as "alternate lovers." To counter the Prime Minister's strategy of shifting coalitions, in mid-1977 the two parties announced the formation of a "democratic convergence," defined as "a substantial understanding among parties having the same concept of democracy, which may or may not be expressed directly as a government platform." But this political understanding proved short-lived; the Social Democrats subsequently gave Soares votes in Parliament both for the agrarian reform and a bill to compensate owners of nationalized property.

If Soares cannot cope with increasingly intractable economic problems, Diogo Freitas do Amaral, the astute head of the CDS, hopes that his party will be invited into the Cabinet as part of a "presidential majority," which will work closely with Eanes. The PSD also looks forward to entering the government.

On the Left, Communist leader Alvaro Cunhal, who scorns the CDS and the PSD as "reactionary fascist forces," once talked wistfully of his party's governing in harness with the Socialists. Since the passage of the agrarian reform, the white-maned Marxist leader has declared his party's complete opposition to the Socialist regime, calling for the dismissal of Parliament, and urging a new national election. Meanwhile, Cunhal has made it clear that the Communists, who dominate Portugal's labor movement and enjoy strong support in the South-Central Alentejo "wheat belt," are prepared to provoke strikes and demonstrations if Soares's policies veer too far to the right. Efforts like the work stoppages called in early 1977 to coincide with the Socialist Prime Minister's visit to major European capitals have been only partially effective, because the PCP lacks full control over the country's workers.

The Popularity of Eanes and Soares

As Soares, perhaps belatedly, seeks solutions to Portugal's economic problems, President Eanes has begun to play a more assertive political role. He garnered a great deal of publicity in May as a result of his participation in the NATO summit meeting in London and his four-day visit to Spain, with which Portugal is developing closer relations. The President seems to have confidence in his understanding of politics and is believed to have encouraged Soares to announce sweeping austerity measures and to bring more technicians into a Cabinet that is short on talent. As he continues regular consultation with key party leaders at Belem Palace, Eanes has obliquely indicated a willingness to reshuffle the Cabinet if economic conditions fail to improve. Even if more technical experts—or representatives of the PSD and CDS—were brought into the government, Soares would no doubt be asked to remain as Prime Minister. According to a public opinion survey published in the July 2, 1977, issue of *Expresso*, a highly respected Lisbon weekly, the Socialist leader remains (along with Eanes) one of the most popular figures in the country.

While sharpening their criticism of the government, the major parties of the Left and Right will avoid obstructionist policies that, in the long run, might discredit the fragile constitutional regime. Portugal's opposition leaders realize that undermining civilian rule could activate the barracks, thereby threatening a return to authoritarianism.

The growing rate of electoral abstention may already betoken some disenchantment with politics. The percentage of eligible voters who failed to cast ballots has risen from 8 percent in the 1975 constituent assembly contests, to 16 percent in the April 1976 parliamentary elections, to 25 percent in the June 1976 presidential balloting, to 35 percent in the December 1976 municipal voting. The decline may also be explained by the fact that voting is no longer a novelty, by the frequency of elections, and by the complicated procedure used in the municipal contests.

At the margin of politics is the military, segments of which toppled the dictatorship and ran the country for 28 months thereafter. The armed forces in Portugal have a more important formal position than in any other West European nation; the 1976 constitution gives their Revolutionary Council the right to "review" or veto actions taken by the National Assembly. Despite this mandate, a confluence of factors has persuaded the council to assume a low profile. First, while dominated by moderates, the Revolutionary Council is riven by philosophical differences and personality conflicts. Second, as chairman, President Eanes has stressed the importance of civilian politicians, while deemphasizing the council's mission. Third, Eanes has prohibited officers from holding both field commands and council posts, a move that has further attenuated the body's influence and has led to the resignation of commands by two Leftist officers. Fourth, the military is now only one-fourth its size at the time of the coup, when 201,000 men were in uniform, and the number may decline further within several years. Although an economic collapse could produce enough political instability to draw the military back into politics, most officers realize that the economic assistance from the United States and West European countries so vital to Portugal's future would be halted if a praetorian regime reemerged in Lisbon.

Social Questions

A need to revise the hastily decreed social laws of the post-coup military regime has greatly complicated Soares's task of governing Portugal. Especially challenging has been his goal of altering reforms with respect to landholding, corporate ownership, and labor unions.

An analysis of Portugal's agrarian problems must begin with a description of the country's two most important farming areas: the "north," the region above the Tagus River that bisects the country; and the "south," which lies below the Tagus. The north, portions of which eluded conquest by the Arabs during their 700-year occupation of Iberia until 1492, is known for its Catholic, conservative pre-industrial values and its opposition to Lisbon's centralizing, modernizing impulses. Its Catholicism is accentuated by the presence at Fatima of a shrine where the Blessed Virgin is widely believed to have spoken to three shepherd children in 1917. This rugged mountainous region is quilted with small, subsistence family farms, whose frugal, cautious owners display a fierce sense of independence much like the French of Britanny and the Vendée. Several crops, including corn, potatoes, and grapes, are raised here and the soil is fairly intensively cultivated. Yet there is substantial underemployment, and both productivity and yearly per-capita income ($285) are low. It was in the north that the movement to oust the pro-Communist government of Premier Vasco Gonçalves began in mid-1975; Gonçalves was forced from office on August 29, 1975.

In contrast, the south is dominated by large grain-producing estates that stretch across much of the region's flat, arid surface. The presence of latifundia, many of which belong to absentee landlords, is explained by climate, terrain, and the decision of the Portuguese monarchy to grant nobles extensive holdings as an incentive to reconquer the south from the Arabs, whose arrival had precipitated the flight of thousands of families to the northern mountains. The Gonçalves regime focused its agrarian reform on the Alentejo by seizing farms in excess of 1,750 acres and by looking the other way when penurious farm workers occupied smaller holdings. Before the Marxist Prime Minister left office, an estimated 2.25 million acres were taken over and organized by PCP militants.

Despite bumper harvests in 1975 and 1976, agricultural output fell precipitously in 1977 as wheat production declined from 600,000 to 320,000 tons. Fearful that their lands would be seized by disgruntled workers, many owners had reduced their plantings for the 1977 harvest; others, anxious to produce, had difficulty obtaining necessary credit for seeds, fertilizer, and equipment. Members of Soviet-type cooperatives formed on expropriated estates lacked the expertise to improve production, often slaughtered breeding stock to provide food for their families, and devoted countless hours to political debate and recriminations. As a result, food imports in 1976 exceeded $775 million, approximately $90 for each of Portugal's 8.5 million inhabitants.

The Socialist government determined that the ill-planned agrarian reform of 1975 would have to be slowed or halted lest imports devour all of the country's meager foreign exchange and gold reserves. Also of concern was growing Communist strength among the Alentejo's downtrodden masses. In September 1976, the government returned 101 small- and medium-sized farms in that region to their owners from whom they had been unlawfully taken. Because of his persistent opposition to the return of properties, Agriculture Minister Antônio Lopes Cardoso resigned on November 3, 1976, and subsequently excoriated Soares for "betraying" the Socialist party's goals. His successor, Antônio Barreto, has shown himself to be a tough political fighter and pragmatist. While reaffirming a commitment to rural reform, the new minister continued to return illegally seized farms, advocated compensation for expropriated estates, raised the minimum size of holdings exempted from the agrarian reform, and suspended credits to agricultural cooperatives until they reveal how monies already allocated to them under the reform program have been used. A highly respected source reports that Barreto's aim is to weaken the collectives, erode the PCP's power base, and promote small- and medium-sized farms like those found in northern Europe.

Restructuring the Industrial Base

Even though most banks, iron and steel firms, and ship-building and transportation companies that were national-ized will remain in government hands, Soares has moved to return some corporations that were illegally taken over during the Gonçalvist period. To stimulate investment and output, Soares hopes to encourage the reentry into Portu-gal of many owners, managers, and entrepreneurs who fled as Leftist workers—often aided and abetted by government officials and the military—took possession of their factories or offices, diminishing productivity and bringing chaos to industrial relations. Despite the new government's assurance that property rights will be restored and respected, it has been difficult to entice industrialists and businessmen back to Iberia from Brazil, South Africa, the United States, and other countries where they are attempting to begin a new life.

The potential for industrial disruption is enhanced by the presence of the Communist-controlled Intersindical, which was recognized by the revolutionary government as Portugal's sole labor confederation. Through workers' com-missions, this organization gained a stranglehold on many industries. Three months after taking office, Soares revoked the law that gave Intersindical its preferred status. He also made it somewhat easier for employers to dismiss workers, established a 40-to 45-hour work week, severely restricted overtime pay, placed tighter controls on the use of sick leave, and limited fringe benefits to 50 percent of an employee's basic wage.

In mid-1977, the Prime Minister secured passage of bills to regulate strikes and workers' commissions. The strike legislation, passed with Communist votes, forbids lockouts and permits peaceful picketing. But employees can no longer demand strike wages, as they did under Gonçalves, and even during legal work stoppages they must provide for security and other essential services. The companion bill, supported by the CDS and the Social Democrats, provides for the election by secret ballot of worker representatives who must be consulted on matters relating to pay and working conditions. While privy to information on their firm's performance, they will be excluded from decisions on the day-to-day management of the company, investment matters, and market policy. These measures have enhanced discipline in the work place, as evidenced by the decline in absenteeism from 25 percent (1976) to eight percent (1977). Still, the majority of Portugal's organized workers are affiliated with Communist unions. Intersindical has simply changed its name to the General Confederation of Portuguese Workers. One of the failures of the governing Socialist party has been its inability to make significant inroads in organized labor. Thus the Communists still control an instrument capable of vexing economic disruption.

Foreign Affairs

The central goal of Portuguese foreign policy is integration into West Europe. The leaders of Portugal, a country long considered a feudal, authoritarian backwater, look forward to the day when they are esteemed as active partners in the continent's political affairs and their nation is a full participant in the European Economic Community (EEC).

That Portugal has created a parliamentary democracy, committed herself to respecting civil liberties, and permitted a free press has impressed leaders throughout West Europe. To express appreciation for the democratic changes and to fortify the Socialist Cabinet against extremist attacks, members of the EEC have made available millions of dollars in assistance through the European Investment Bank. On September 22, 1976, Portugal was admitted as the nineteenth member of the Council of Europe, often described as the "conscience of European democracies."

Greater Portuguese participation in NATO has also been encouraged. Because of the African wars, which prompted the United States and several European states to slap an arms embargo on Portugal, the dictatorship failed to meet its nominal commitment of two divisions to NATO. Soon after the 1974 coup, the country was excluded from NATO's Nuclear Planning Group because of the presence of Communists in key positions. With the advent of the Soares regime, Washington and Bonn began to supply armor, training planes and jet fighters. They recognize that the Portuguese army, West Europe's only force with extensive battlefield experience, must convert its capability from jungle warfare to the defense of the continent against a westward lunge by the Warsaw Pact nations. Crucial to this role is a Portuguese airborne brigade, which can be deployed anywhere in West Europe in a few hours.

What are the prospects for Portugal's entry into the Common Market? On September 20, 1976, Foreign Minister José Medeiros Ferreira informed his EEC counterparts that his country wished to become a member as soon as possible —a goal reiterated the following February when Soares toured the capitals of the nine Community members. While anxious to loft the star of Portuguese democracy, the Common Market members will probably postpone deliberations on Portugal's membership until 1978, when it can be considered along with the applications of Greece and Spain. Assuming that favorable action is taken, up to 10 years may be required before the Lisbon regime achieves full membership. A long transitional period is required for Portugal's economy—especially her agrarian sector and small- and medium-sized companies—to meet the competition that tariff removal would entail.

United States Assistance

Complementary needs have drawn Portugal and the United States closer together: the former desperately requires economic assistance; the latter wants to promote order along the western flank of the Mediterranean rim that may be destabilized by a Leftist victory in the 1978 French elections, the increasing importance of the Communist party in Italy, and the possibility of upheaval in Yugoslavia when Marshal Tito dies. Indeed, United States President Gerald Ford termed the emergence of democracy in Portugal a "success" for American foreign policy during an October 8, 1976, debate with Democratic presidential nominee Jimmy Carter. Washington has poured millions of dollars into Lisbon to keep the Portuguese economy from collapsing. During fiscal year 1977, the United States government made available to Portugal $300 million in temporary credits, $70 million in Public Law 480 surplus agricultural products, $60 million in development grants and loans, and $32.25 million in military assistance. For fiscal year 1978, President Carter, who has written other industrial powers urging support for Portugal's Socialist government, has supported legislation to provide $300 million in medium-term aid (to assist Portugal with balance-of-payments problems) and $25 million in military aid.

Soares demonstrated his appreciation for United States assistance by assuring the Americans that they could continue to use the Lajes base in the Azores and by increasing his country's participation in NATO, a move urged by the Portuguese military, which hopes for higher professional status and a clear European defense role. Washington was also pleased by Lisbon's decision to elevate its diplomatic representation in Israel to the ambassadorial level. This initiative, which brought loud grumbles from the Arab nations on which energy-poor Portugal is dependent, was apparently motivated by Soares's commitment to the program of the Socialist International, which endorses full relations with Israel. Foreign Minister Medeiros Ferreira defended the step as an "act of sovereignty," noting that Portuguese embassies have been opened in 30 countries—including the Soviet Union— since 1974.

With respect to Portugal's erstwhile African territories, ties with Angola are improving, and relations with Guinea-Bissau, Cape Verde and Sao Tome have been termed "excellent." In contrast, the Foreign Minister characterizes relations with Mozambique as "bad." This negative assessment springs from the Maputo regime's massive expulsion of whites—over 600,000 refugees, most of whom came from Angola, have entered Portugal from Africa in the last three years—and Lisbon's subsequent noncompliance with pledges to provide economic and technical assistance to its former colony. Further complicating the relationship is the presence in Portugal of the Mozambique United Front, an organization dedicated to the overthrow of the African state's radical government.

Conclusion

In view of a protracted dictatorship that fostered monopolies, established captive African markets, suppressed labor activities and squandered billions of escudos on a debilitating colonial war, Portugal's problems are no surprise. What is surprising is the country's ability to stay afloat economically while a parliamentary democracy takes root. Principal credit for these achievements must be given to Mário Soares's consummate skill at political compromise with groups on the Left and Right and inside his own Socialist party. But the country's political development will continue only if economic conditions improve; and improvement is contingent on the willingness of the long-suffering Portuguese people to submit themselves to severe austerity measures and the readiness of Portugal's allies to furnish large amounts of foreign assistance.

TROUBLED PORTUGAL [2]

Official Washington is a bit gloomy about Portugal these days. As one State Department functionary put it bluntly the other day: "It looks as if Portugal is going down the drain." But it would be a pity to write off Lisbon's democratic experiment too soon.

[2] Article by Kenneth Maxwell, associate professor of history at Columbia University. New York *Times.* p 37. Mr. 8, '78. © 1978 by The New York Times Company. Reprinted by permission.

It remains a matter of extreme importance to the West that democracy in Portugal succeed. The consequences of a return to a rightist authoritarian role would profoundly disturb the whole of Southern Europe. It would confirm the prediction of Alvaro Cunhal, the Portuguese Communist leader, that Portugal's economic and social structure cannot support a parliamentary regime. Moreover, the prestige of the United States has been repeatedly committed to the success of the democratic experiment, and the failure of the constitutional regime would be a major blow.

But what are the chances for Portuguese democracy? The problems are formidable. The economic situation is precarious. Inflation is the highest in Europe. Over 15 percent of the working population is unemployed; the percentage of underemployed is much higher. The balance of payments is in chronic deficit, vital imports of foods and export-related materials are financed with emergency foreign loans and credits. The government's operating deficits are enormous and cannot be sustained. The population is threatened with a substantial lowering in recently raised living standards, always historically a dangerous circumstance. There is much disillusion with the political class's incompetence, pettiness and corruption. The schools and universities remain disorganized, as they have been for four years.

There have been a mountain of projects, proposals, laws, but very little action. The bureaucracy is reeling after four years of purges, cronyism, overmanning, changes of direction, and a chronic absence of modern managerial abilities. The military remains deeply involved in politics. The parties, except possibly the Communists, face increasing tensions between leadership and rank-and-file.

The organized working class will bear the brunt of the austerity measures required by Portugal's creditors, and the role of the Socialists in implementing these measures will further undermine their working-class support and add to that of the Communists.

Among the poorer, less-organized sectors of the population, many already go hungry; more are likely to do so.

There is a revival of overtly fascist and ultraright sentiment and organization. The feeling of anxiety and insecurity among the general public in the face of rising crime and drug use continues to grow. The government's freedom of action is severely curtailed, and is seen to be so. The role of foreigners and foreign *diktats* in Portuguese policy, especially economic policy, is increasingly resented.

The Positive Signs

But there are positive elements. For the first time since the new Constitution came into operation, in 1976, the government is assured a clear parliamentary majority. The agreement between the Socialists and the Center Democrats, if it holds, and provided both parties can maintain internal discipline in the National Assembly, should guarantee passage of the government's economic austerity program. Hence, negotiations with the International Monetary Fund can be resumed, and presumably the "great loan," as the Portuguese call it, will be forthcoming.

The important point is that the nearly $750 million loan package that the United States has played a leading role in putting together (its contribution would be $300 million) would buy some breathing space—not long, but at least enough for a planned, rather than a catastrophic, retrenchment to take hold and, with luck, for economic recovery to begin.

And there are other positive signs. Emigrant remittances, always a critical booster of Portugal's economic fortunes, are again at a high level. Tourism is improving. The first constitutional crisis was surmounted without recourse to extra-constitutional means. The role of the President, General Ramalho Eanes, was critical in this because he remained firm in support of a political-party and democratic solution to the crisis. The antidemocratic right is voluble but still lacks national leadership.

The Center Democrats, which in the European context are basically a conservative and Christian-democratic type of party, have recognized that any government, whatever its political coloration, must pursue similar policies in Portugal's present situation.

They have risked sharing the onus for unpopular measures in the national interest, and they have also risked alienating their supporters in the country because the agreement with the Socialists is just as distasteful to the Center Democrats' electoral constituency as an agreement with the conservatives is to that of the Socialists'. Both parties at considerable ideological cost have put the nation first. What Portugal needs most now is some confidence—in herself, and from her friends. It is not the time to write off the hopes of a democratic future.

PORTUGAL TURNS TO THE RIGHT [3]

In everyday national life, the new mood in Portugal is particularly noticeable in the schools. Even in the southern city of Beja, a major Communist stronghold, the Center Democrats have taken over many of the student councils, only recently dominated by the Communists and far Left.

One conservative teacher attributed this to a desire by the youth for stability after four years of revolutionary pandemonium in the classrooms. A youth councillor in the same city felt the rising CDS influence was due to its offering the students greater freedom at all levels. He saw this was true in his own youth center where "before, all you could hear was endless revolutionary music, which stopped the students coming. Now they can pick their own records. They've all come back."

Galloping inflation, rampant unemployment and now, a tax-laden budget, have all combined to produce a growing swing of public opinion in Portugal—to the right.

At the government level the composition of the ruling coalition reflects the shift in the mood.

The Socialists, who shunned the conservative Center

[3] From "Portuguese in Sharp Swing Toward the Right," by Helen Gibson, special correspondent. *Christian Science Monitor.* p 5. Mr. 20, '78. Reprinted by permission from *The Christian Science Monitor.* © 1978 The Christian Science Publishing Society. All rights reserved.

Democrats (CDS) as extreme rightists and even fascists, in the hot revolutionary summer of 1975, have taken them on as partners—albeit junior ones—in their newly formed second constitutional government. Socialist Prime Minister Mário Soares now describes them as "patriotic centrists."

In the industrial city of Setubal a teacher at a high school which has recently gone conservative cited the "intransigence and demagoguery of the leftists who promised the students things they knew beforehand they could never fulfill."

An ugly manifestation of this trend has been a sudden wave of Nazi swastikas and posters of the former dictator, Antonio Salazar, appearing in a number of high schools around the country. One Lisbon high school was closed recently after violent clashes between young Communists and students wearing the insignia of a far right party.

In Northern Oporto, a group of students at the Garcia Orta high school plastered the walls with swastikas, sang old Portuguese fascist hymns, and stoned the teachers' room windows in protest at what they considered the teachers' left-wing views.

In Lisbon's expensive modern high-sector, graffiti spelling "death to the Communists" has suddenly appeared. A young American sociologist who mixes with university students said it had become "chic among young people to be a Nazi, especially among the middle- and upper-class brackets where the youth are trying to shock the establishment." In 1975, the in-thing for these young people to do was to join the wild, Maoist MRP party.

A previously unknown extreme right group claimed responsibility for a fire that gutted the science faculty building of Lisbon's university over the weekend. An anonymous caller claiming to represent the "command for the defense of western civilization" told the national news agency ANOP the fire would be followed by similar attacks on other faculties and schools.

He said the attack was launched to demand the release of right-wingers arrested for bomb attacks in 1975 and to protest against the conservative Center Democrats' decision to join in a coalition government with the Socialists.

Most observers agree that such manifestations represent the fringe, hooligan elements of the new mood. This was illustrated in a recent Lisbon march organized by the moderate right to protest the rising disenchantment of the middle classes over their salaries, frozen since the coup of 1974.

Thousands of middle-class couples and families were joined by about a dozen young thugs in motorcycle crash helmets who took the head of the march and triggered clashes outside the Communist headquarters that happened to be on the route.

Books by personalities of the old Salazar regime also are enjoying a sudden success. Bookstore managers attribute it partly to curiosity about an era that was tightly closed off from public scrutiny and partly to disillusion with the present economic situation—one where spiraling prices, unemployment, and lack of housing has affected every part of the population.

PORTUGAL'S HIGH LIVING COSTS [4]

The Portuguese, who never had it especially good, are fast learning the meaning of the word austerity. Portugal's third punitive budget since Mr. Mário Soares became prime minister in 1976 was passed by parliament on April 13th. The budget is a further attempt to cut the country's ruinous balance of payments deficit, which last year rose to $1.4 billion. Portugal's finance minister, Mr. Vitor Constancio, hopes his measures will impress the International Monetary Fund enough to release $800 million in international loans.

The wage rises which followed the fall of the old regime four years ago have long been wiped out by spectacular price increases. Prices have become a national obsession. Music broadcasts have been replaced by experts explaining how soya can make meat go further. Housewives are telling each

[4] From "We Never Had It So Bad," by the Lisbon correspondent. The Economist. 267:69. Ap. 22, '78. © The Economist Newspaper Ltd., London, 1978. Reprinted with permission.

other about the nutritional value of parsley and garlic soup.

Last year the price of food and drink alone rose by more than 25 percent after the escudo was devalued and import taxes were raised. Since 1974 many items have doubled or quadrupled in price, if they can be found at all. Prunes, for instance, now cost more than 10 times what they did four years ago. Bananas and pineapples, once cheap and plentiful, are exotic luxuries. Portugal used to be a fish-eating nation, but in four years popular staples like hake and squid have quadrupled in price, and shellfish is totally out of reach. Canteen cooks offer fresh trout, which is still reasonably priced, but workers have been infuriated by this enforced change in their diet. Queues appear wherever dried salt cod, a popular dish, appears on sale. The government reluctantly agreed to import cod at inflated prices for the traditional Christmas eve dinner last year, but insisted it would be the last time. Subsidies for imported beef have now been cut and pork, an unpopular dish in the hot summer months, will be the cheapest meat.

Nothing seems to be sacred. Wine has nearly doubled in price, although by British standards it still costs next to nothing. Spare parts are running out and washing machines and dishwashers in many households are immobilized. Even the sun is becoming scarce. The Portuguese are being eased out of the holiday spots by visitors from abroad bearing precious foreign exchange as travel agents make block bookings. Families determined to spend their traditional Easter holiday on the coast of the southern Algarve this year had to book their hotels through friends abroad.

Relatively well-off middle-class families with net incomes of £250 a month are selling old books and jewelry and doing without their daily helps. Nine-tenths of the population earns between £70 and £120 a month, which leaves little room for maneuver. Wage increases of up to 20 percent and extra social security benefits have been promised. But income tax has gone up at least a tenth for most people, and a new sales tax will push up prices of non-subsidized foods in the coming months. Electricity and transport charges have also gone up sharply. All told, most families will find their living standards cut by as much as a third.

Last year's increases were received with stoic resignation. "We are slow to anger and we can put up with a lot," one newspaper editor said recently. "But when things reach a certain stage, then we can suddenly explode."

Cheating the State

Cheating the state has long been a popular diversion. Now it is becoming a necessity. The government complains that billions of escudos leave the country every day as families cross the border for a day's shopping in Spanish department stores and come back laden with shellfish, bananas, instant coffee and shoes. Television sets and other electronic goods are smuggled in by bribing customs officers. Top political figures are said to be involved in smuggling in coffee from Angola. Frozen beef is illegally brought in from Argentina and housewives with friendly grocers can get contrabrand items under the counter. Repairmen add a chunk to the bill if the customer demands a receipt.

Trained sub-managers and skilled workers are demanding big salary increases and proposing to look for jobs in America or Brazil. Other workers threaten to bring several large companies to a standstill if such increases are granted. Punitive interest rates now being worked out between the government and the IMF could, it is feared, bankrupt many small firms and throw hundreds of thousands of people out of work.

The full impact of the new measures has yet to make itself felt. Demonstrations being staged this month against the high cost of living still attract only small crowds. Enough drivers can afford Europe's highest petrol prices (£1.54 a gallon) to throng the streets. Restaurants have kept prices stable by quietly cutting the size of their portions, and are still doing good business. The rise in household bills will not come through until the end of May. There could be trouble then.

DENATIONALIZING PORTUGUESE BUSINESS FIRMS [5]

Soon after the left-wing revolution of April 25, 1974, employes of Companhia Portuguesa de Amidos, a starch-making company based in this Lisbon suburb [of Sacavem, Portugal] took over the management, seizing virtually all power from the boss, Victor M. Carmona e Costa.

Mr. Carmona e Costa could still show up every day if he wanted to, but he wasn't treated with much deference and his workday consisted mainly of writing an occasional check and sulking.

Under the workers' control, the firm, like most of the 300 other Portuguese companies taken over by employes, ran into operating and financial trouble. Finally the workers' committee booted out Mr. Carmona e Costa entirely. At the workers' request, the state intervened and assumed responsibility for the firm.

Today the company, known as Copam, is "75 percent back to where it was before the revolution," according to its president. Salaries have been raised by 20 percent since last April. Three round-the-clock shifts are producing 100 tons of starch a day, still not enough to meet increasing demand. The company is making profit, and is building an addition to increase capacity by 50 percent.

The man directing the recovery: Victor M. Carmona e Costa, the former boss.

Process of Disintervention

Copam is typical of the small-to medium-sized businesses taken over by employes after the revolution and now being given back to their owners. At Sanimar Ltd. in Lisbon, Virgilio Esteves is back from Brazil and once again in charge of his building-contracting and home-appliance business. José Machado has returned as president of Guerin Ltd., a

[5] From "Portuguese Businessmen Back on the Job As the Government Returns Their Firms," by Philip Revzin, staff reporter. *Wall Street Journal.* p 34. Ja. 13, '78. Reprinted by permission of The Wall Street Journal. © 1978 Dow Jones & Company, Inc. All rights reserved.

big auto assembler and garage operator, after being idle for more than a year. Bernardo de Almeida, the Count of Caria, is also back at work, heading up a number of businesses, including Coca-Cola's Portuguese unit.

Most of the businesses that had been taken over foundered because of the recession, the inexperience of the worker management, and economic problems caused by the sudden loss of Portugal's colonies in Africa. The state intervened by appointing its own managers to try to bail out the firms, but for the past year the Socialists have been calling back the former owners. This process, known as "disintervention," is still only about half complete.

The firms being given back were never formally nationalized, but many larger firms were. The government nationalized a huge chunk—60 percent—of Portuguese industry, including the banks, shipbuilding, oil and chemicals, most of which had been owned by a few wealthy, old-line families. These industrialists, who were closely tied to the old dictatorship of Antonio Salazar, aren't likely to return soon, at least not to their old companies.

José Manuel de Mello and his brother Jorge, for instance, whose CUF group of companies was nationalized, remain in London and Switzerland respectively, although José was recently reelected president of the Lisnave shipyard and retains an interest in the yard. Property owners like the de Mellos whose land or companies were seized have asked for millions of dollars in compensation under a new law, and they may eventually be paid.

The disintervention of the smaller firms and the return of the entrepreneurs have a lot to do with the current political crisis in Portugal. The Socialist government of Prime Minister Mário Soares felt it had to give the firms back to try to stem growing economic chaos. The problems, dating from before the revolution, included a growing dependence on imports of oil and consumer goods, and therefore a rapidly increasing balance-of-payments deficit, the lack of a solid industrial base and inefficient use of the country's vast farm land.

The Socialists wanted to revive small- and medium-sized industry as a first step toward an industrial revival. But disintervention only added to Mr. Soares's political problems. The right-wing and centrist parties said the policy didn't go far enough to restore the confidence of businessmen or foreign investors. The sizable Communist Party and the trade unions called it a "betrayal" of gains made during the revolution.

Government Topples

Faced with pressure to institute austere budget measures to bring down the balance-of-payments deficit, and to forge a political consensus to satisfy the International Monetary Fund and other potential creditors, Mr. Soares asked for a vote of confidence for his policies in the National Assembly December 8 [1977]. With the two right-wing parties against him, and the last-minute opposition of the Communists, Mr. Soares lost the vote by 159 to 100 and immediately resigned.

He now heads a caretaker regime and has been asked to form a new government. He and many other politicians are warning that a consensus on economic policy must be reached soon, to avoid violence from the extreme right- and left-wing factions still operating in the country.

Portuguese business, much of which wasn't affected either by nationalization or intervention, wants disintervention to proceed quickly. "A lot of these companies were having trouble in 1974 because of the world-wide recession," says Antonio Vasco de Mello, president of the Confederation of Portuguese Industry. "Also, many of them had been mismanaged. Intervention at first was a sound policy, aimed at rescuing companies short of nationalization. But in 1975, for political reasons, it began to be abused. Now, as the economy shows signs of recovery, the state should rapidly pull out so these companies can get healthier."

Copam illustrates the problems of takeovers. The 45-year-old firm, which is 28 percent owned by Dutch interests, has a virtual monopoly on starch production in Portugal. It supplies starch and glucose as raw materials for a number of industries. Mr. Carmona e Costa, who has worked for the company for 25 years, says that before the revolution "the company had a huge profit, no debts, and warehouses packed with goods to be shipped."

A Prisoner in My Office

But from April 1974 to July 1975, Mr. Carmona e Costa says, "I was a prisoner in my office. They needed me to sign the checks, but I couldn't make any decisions." The chief engineer says that he, too, was kept in his small office all day. And technicians, now busy checking starch formulas, say the atmosphere in the factory was one of "anarchy."

For nearly a year Copam was run by a workers' committee of 14 employes. Mr. Carmona e Costa concedes that the factory was showing a profit, but he says the workers were simply selling off already-completed product and weren't launching projects or lining up new business. He claims that the workers' committee obtained a $375,000 bank loan and that the money "has never been accounted for satisfactorily." (The workers say they obtained no such loan; in fact, they say, they paid off $150,000 in debts previously run up by the firm.) Mr. Carmona e Costa also says that when he returned to his old office, he found liquor in the filing cabinets "and strange bills, like 80,000 escudos ($2,000) for dog meat one month."

On July 28, 1975, the workers' committee asked the government to intervene and appoint new managers. Mr. Carmona e Costa was given 15 minutes to clear out of his office. He went first to Spain and then to Brazil, where he acted as a consultant to a new starch factory there. He says that even though he was earning a salary about double the $875 a month he made at Copam, life was hard in Brazil and his wife had to work as a sales clerk in a glass shop to make ends meet.

Mission to Brazil

In the late summer of 1976, the newly elected Mr. Soares went to Brazil to persuade exiled businessmen to return to Portugal. Mr. Carmona e Costa was among those who listened and came back. Some businessmen were more reluctant. Mr. Esteves of Sanimar, the builders, was sent the keys to his factory by the minister of industry and told to take the factory back. He says he suspected that the workers' group had looted the company of more than $2 million in assets and he refused to come back until an accounting was made. "I sent the keys right back to them," he says. He was finally persuaded to return. (Mr. Esteves never got his accounting, or any compensation, and he is suing the government for the $2 million.)

Mr. Carmona e Costa insisted that he be able to fire some of the workers, and he negotiated with the government over how he could run his firm. He finally returned to Copam last July 27, amid controversy. The workers still in control of the plant didn't want him back. For two days workers blocked the gate and prevented him from entering. On the third attempt, escorted by armed police, the boss got in.

Then he faced a plant that was half on strike, "and I was only able to go into one small office, in a section of the factory where the maintenance men, who supported me, had control." For the next two months, he says, "we fought a war of attrition; we had to win back our factory section by section, bit by bit." During that time, he goes on, "we would peer out of the Venetian blinds at militants with long knives, who were terrorizing the secretaries." (The unions and the Communist Party hotly deny that any of their supporters had knives.) Demonstrations of up to 700 people outside the gates were common.

Mr. Carmona e Costa was himself an issue in the controversy. The unions say he had close ties to the Salazar regime and was a difficult, insensitive boss. They also say he mismanaged the company and left $250,000 in debts, a charge he denies. He concedes that salaries were too low.

Sixteen Suspended

Now, Mr. Carmona e Costa says, the entire plant is under his control, and working well again. After his return he suspended 16 workers he says were the worst troublemakers.

(Under Portugal's current law, it is difficult to fire employes; the 16 Copam workers are suspended with pay until their cases are reviewed in the courts.) He also raised wages, which were essentially frozen during the workers' control, by 20 percent retroactive to April.

Mr. Carmona e Costa says that all this has been hard on him and his wife ("Strange cars would drive past our house at all hours, making our dogs bark") and on many of the plant employes, some of whom had been with Copam for more than 20 years. "It was just a core group of Communists that made us a target case," he says.

To protect his loyal staff, he says, he hired three large bodyguards, veterans of Portuguese involvement in the former colonies of Angola and Mozambique. The unions call these men "hired thugs, there to terrorize the workers." The men drive Mr. Carmona e Costa to and from work in a big black Mercedes and search all visitors.

On a stroll through the factory's lush gardens, Mr. Carmona e Costa shows a visitor a headless statue of a woman in long-flowing robes. The statue was beheaded by the workers, he says. (The workers say the vandalism was perpetrated by Mr. Carmona e Costa's "thugs.")

In the main computer control room, a workman who Mr. Carmona e Costa says is a Communist, but not one of the ringleaders of the takeover, sits eating a beans-and-rice lunch. Pasted to one of the computer consoles is a statement issued by the workers' committee last year, urging: "Comrades, take care of the machines; each wasted bag of starch means lower wages for all of us." As the boss enters, the worker politely stands up, greets him and chats for a few minutes.

"Two months ago he was throwing stones at my car," Mr. Carmona e Costa says. "Now he asks me how my wife is feeling."

PORTUGAL'S FOREIGN ECONOMIC NEEDS [6]

As the fourth anniversary of Portugal's revolution approaches, its celebrations will be muted. The country is finally having to come to grips with its yawning balance of payments gap and growing debt. After running a current deficit of $1 billion in 1975 and $1.2 billion in 1976, the government had hoped to make a start in getting it down. Instead, the hoped for reduced deficit of $800 millions last year turned into another $1.2 billion gap. A massive 60 percent increase in its import bill put paid to these hopes despite a recovery in tourism and worker remittances. Only 40 percent of imports are now being covered by exports.

The country's well-publicized gold reserves (860 tons) have kept the country afloat. This asset is now virtually exhausted. Sixty tons have already been disposed of, while much of the rest has been pledged as collateral against loans. Moreover, although technically worth a considerable sum, it remains to be seen how liquid these assets would be at free market prices in the event of obligatory disposal. By any conceivable reckoning the payments deficit will persist for a number of years. Accordingly, sizeable international help is vital.

The price, however, is a stiff dose of patented IMF retrenchment medicine. The international organization has itself offered a mere $50 millions repeat of an earlier loan worth the same amount. But contingent on this loan, itself contingent on adherence to the IMF conditions, is a $750 millions OECD consortium loan. To get this, Portugal has been pressed to agree to a further devaluation, a draconian halving of food imports (though last year's food crop was a near-disaster), public spending cuts, a credit squeeze, and a cutback in GNP growth targets to around 3½ percent (recovery targets would be a more appropriate term).

All this, it is hoped, will begin to close the payments gap,

[6] From "Portugal: Victim of Dogma," by Basil Caplan, contributing editor. *The Banker.* 128:35-7. Mr. '78. © The Financial Times Limited 1978. Reprinted from The Banker with the Editor's permission.

starting with a reduction to $800 millions this year. But the question is increasingly being asked whether this is the appropriate recipe for a country with Portugal's type of economy. To the hapless Portuguese it looks rather like a catch-22, no-win situation. In straight bookkeeping terms it may look right: cut imports, increase exports, or import substitutes, and all will come out right. In practice, apart from the feasibility of cutting essential imports, the very success in doing so may also put paid to hopes of boosting exports.

The argument for cutting imports is that the country is unnecessarily importing luxuries and optional extras. In fact, imports in this category play a relatively minor role. As one of Portugal's leading bankers points out, in recent years luxury imports have accounted for around seven percent of the nation's bill. Far outweighing imports of cars and the like are foodstuffs, capital goods, raw materials and essential oil supplies. With exceedingly low levels of agricultural productivity, the country has to import more than half its food, despite the fact that half the population lives on the land. And without imports of capital goods and energy sources, the country's industry can, at best, stagnate.

This leads on to the no-win situation. Undoubtedly, Portugal's not infertile land is capable of making the country far more self-sufficient than it is at present. But the key inevitably lies in greater imports of agricultural machinery and fertilizers. And if this is to be paid with greater manufactured exports more, not less, capital goods imports are needed. As a further twist, it so happens that Portugal's main manufactured exports are textiles (25–30 percent of the total). Besides being undercapitalized, the universally unloved textile industry also runs up against another problem, that of customer-imposed import restrictions (by the UK among others). Two of Portugal's German-owned textile companies have recently gone into liquidation.

In terms of the domestic economy, a policy of stringent credit restrictions is expected to bring about a spreading pool of bankrupt companies. For the last few years, hundreds of smaller companies from the private sector have been kept alive under the protective umbrella of government subsidies. It is generally acknowledged that it is these private companies which offer the best hope for exports. Without benefit of further credit restrictions, industry as a whole is already estimated to be operating at no more than 75 percent capacity.

Arguably, the credit squeeze can be so tailored as to curtail domestic consumption and boost export industry. In practice, this may prove difficult. Given the political constraints on curbing spending by the large public sector, the private sector exporters seem destined to take the cutting edge.

Invisible earnings from tourism and worker remittances will at least benefit from a devaluation, but they cannot be expected to do more than alleviate the trade imbalance.

The Threat to Democracy

The second part of the saga leads on to the social implications of the retrenchment. Unemployment, at least 15 percent (the scale of underemployment has yet to be adequately quantified), is already at warning light level, while real wages are estimated to have dropped 18 percent. The fact that Portugal's infant parliamentary democracy has got through the past 18 months and taken politics off the streets is scarcely sufficient to allow complacency.

The recently formed *de facto* coalition between Mário Soares's Socialist Party and the conservative CDS party of Freitas do Amaral will certainly ensure greater parliamentary stability. But it is questionable whether it will be proof against a further dose of deflation. The 16 percent vote secured by the Communists is no true measure of their strength. Two-thirds of the Communist vote is concentrated in the impoverished southern Alentejo (also the country's bread-basket), and in the industrial belt around Lisbon. The political poll-watchers foresee their share of the vote increasing, alongside further defections from the left-wing of the Socialist party. At the same time, the moderate Socialists have so far failed in their bid to wean the trade unions from the Communist Intersindical. Accordingly, the left has a strong, concentrated base, both geographically and industrially. Far from speaking the language of Eurocommunism, Communist leader Alvaro Cunhal continues to speak in terms of the 1974–75 revolution, equating resuscitation of the private sector with the old Salazar regime.

On the other side of the political spectrum, the conservative forces in the nation, including supporters of the *ancien regime*, are largely concentrated in the northern half of the country. The potential for a risky geographical split between the two halves of the country cannot be dismissed. With this political configuration, a purely deflationary financial solution to the country's problems may appear somewhat simplistic.

A New Marshall Plan?

The alternative would be a recognition that a country like Portugal should be given the means to ride out its payment deficits and continue to expand with the help of a Marshall Plan type of assistance. In this context, it is worth recalling that some of the wealthy countries now demanding strict retrenchment as the price of the $750 millions loan, themselves achieved their postwar "miracle economies" thanks, first and foremost, to the said Marshall Plan at the end of World War II.

It is also highly pertinent to the present-day world trade stagnation that the United States, donor of the Marshall Plan, was also motivated by a degree of enlightened self-interest, benefiting its own economy while helping a war-torn Europe to get on its feet. The suggestion that there may be something cynical in the way the world's have-nations have lost their enthusiasm for massively aiding plucky little Portugal, promising a warm welcome into the Common Market, etc., would doubtless be indignantly refuted. Yet, a couple of years ago, the OECD consortium, sponsored by Henry Kissinger, was talking liberally of a $1.5 billion loan, if only Portugal would stick to the straight and narrow path.

Today that loan, long delayed, has been cut to $750 millions. And the warm welcome into the Common Market? The most recent word is that the Commission's opinion on Portugal's application would be "slightly delayed because of recent political events."

If the idealism of yester-year has evaporated, the same enlightened self-interest which motivated the original Marshall Plan might at least carry greater weight. Portugal's problems may have been exacerbated by its political turmoil and the loss of its African empire. But in the last analysis, they stem from the same causes—the massive increase in oil prices and general trade stagnation—as are playing havoc with the economies of most poor and underdeveloped countries. The catch-22 situation applies too, perhaps, globally: impose retrenchment on the indebted have-nots and, in so doing, shrink the export markets of the industrialized countries, and in so doing . . . Is the dogma of balanced payments really the answer?

PORTUGAL'S UNEASY CATHOLIC CHURCH [7]

Portugal has just acquired a new, revolutionary set of civil laws, and the Roman Catholic Church is extremely unhappy about many aspects of them.

Under the new code, which set out to revise thoroughly the laws ordained by the previous, 50-year-old fascist regime, married couples can adopt either the man's or the woman's surname, the most guilty party in a divorce or separation case is responsible for family support, and women, for the first time, are entirely free to take up a job without first having their husband's permission.

In years past, the law saw the woman's place as in the home and made sure she remained in it. Most rules favored the male. A woman, for instance, could be jailed for up to

[7] From "Portugal's Roman Catholic Church Uneasy Over New Civil Laws," by Helen Gibson, special correspondent. *Christian Science Monitor.* p 4. My. 5, '78.

a year for opening her husband's mail, while a husband could read his wife's because she was regarded as "under his authority."

Again, a woman, unless she had taken the precautions of legally separating her possessions at the time of her wedding, gave up all claims to administering any property or business she brought with her into the marriage. The husband virtually could do what he liked with it.

Then came the 1974 revolution, and a Constitution that abolished all types of discrimination between the sexes, religious beliefs, races, or creeds. The laws were dragged out, worked over with a fine-tooth comb, and a new code written.

The church's dismay was triggered by the attitude of the code to the family. In a pastoral letter, Catholic bishops bitterly attacked the new laws for emphasizing the principle of equality between legitimate children and those born out of wedlock.

"This weakens the link given to marriage by children," the bishops said.

Under the old laws, illegitimate children were penalized. They were not allowed to inherit more than one-third of the father's estate if there were any legitimate children around, and they could join neither the church nor the military. Because of its strict divorce laws, Portugal in the early 1970s with a population of around nine million numbered around 1.5 million such children.

The church also criticized what it called "exaggerated and formalistic regulations [in the new code] concerning the principle of equality of the sexes in a married couple." This, said the bishops, would encourage family dissension and the consequent recourse to the law courts, with all the inevitable damage to the spontaneity and intimacy of domestic life.

For most Portuguese women, however, the new Constitution, with its abolition of all discrimination, represents the best thing the revolution has brought them.

"We must reinforce women in all kinds of associations— local, political, trade unions. Otherwise, Portugal will again revert to marginalizing them," says Teresa Ambrosio, a Socialist Party deputy to the National Assembly and a mother of four. "It is difficult for us, because we are Mediterranean, Catholic, and more conservative, and the previous regime repressed our development. But we must work at it."

PORTUGAL'S PRESS AT A CROSSROADS [8]

When Portugal's military junta nationalized the banks in March 1975, it became the reluctant guardian of eight bank-owned national daily newspapers. True to its vow to permit free expression after 42 dismal years of rigid censorship, the government has been propping these papers up to the tune of $2 million a month, a heavy investment in an impoverished country. And the state-owned press also has been something of an embarrassment to the moderate and freely elected but shaky Socialist government now in power.

After a commission reported on months of study and public debate, the government announced this fall that it would no longer pick up the bills and would authorize salary cuts and layoffs. It also wondered whether it should hand back three papers to their original owners. But some editors remained skeptical that the council of ministers had the strength and will to move resolutely against opposition from the papers, the workers and a multitude of clamorous political factions. If it does, some of the papers doubtless will go under.

The capital, Lisbon, a city of only 800,000, has three morning and five evening newspapers. Oporto, the second largest city, with 300,000 population, has three mornings. One of the three morning papers and three of the five evening papers in Lisbon and two of the three in Oporto are state-owned in full or in part. As in the less-developed countries, there are no papers of any consequence of the smaller cities. This is another factor the government considers worri-

[8] Article by Milton Hollstein, professor of communication, University of Utah, Salt Lake City. *Nieman Reports.* 31:55-6. Summer/Autumn '77. Copyright © 1977 by the President and Fellows of Harvard College. Reprinted with permission.

some. For the moment it has the upper hand over the far left, and it is pledged to building a democratic public opinion among the once-inert populace of nine million.

The year-old constitution contains lengthy guarantees of personal rights but forbids private ownership of television. Most radio and all television were nationalized earlier, but television is primitive and the government-appointed managers are struggling against the daily disruptions by Communist-run unions.

Two newspapers were suspended previously but their plants and other assets were kept intact and their staffs still were being paid, since it is difficult and unpopular to fire anyone in Portugal.

Even more bizarre is that the government, because it is pledged to "pluralism" of opinion, has been supporting papers of a wide political spectrum, including some that regularly attack it. Two of the state-owned papers are closely allied to the Communist Party, although the government got rid of Communist dominance in most of the press in a shakeup following an aborted left-wing counter-coup in November 1975. Oddly, too, one of the few papers believed to be in the black is the pro-Communist *Diario Popular*, a well-edited evening paper in Lisbon with about 68,000 circulation. Its tone is a marked contrast to the strident *O Diario*, the non-governmental organ of the Communist Party.

Newspapers Right and Left

That Portugal has a free press at all is remarkable. Today print media of every political coloration flood the country and are available at kiosks eveywhere. Yet the nation has known only brief periods of such freedom. From the time the dictator Antonio Salazar clamped down in 1926 until the coup of April 1974, all forms of expression were rigidly controlled. Salazar's successor in 1968, Marcelo Caetano, effected some liberalization but profoundly disappointed the press by failing to end censorship.

Immediately after the 1974 coup the press, which had

been predictably spoonfed, bland, and almost entirely compliant, indulged in an orgy of what one press elder statesman called "gratuitous accusation, complaints, uncontained hatred and vile demonstrations." The result was that the provisional government, the first of six, issued a tough press law. Three newspapers were suspended briefly and one, *Luta Popular*, the mouthpiece of the Maoist MRPP, indefinitely.

Among the independent national newspapers are seven weeklies. These weeklies were an especially important balance wheel during the fitful summer of 1975, when a Communist-leaning triumvirate was in power under the Armed Forces Movement, and their circulations boomed. They represent a wider graduation of opinion to the right of the Communists. At the extreme right is *A Rua*, which supports the discredited Salazar policies. All but one sprouted since the revolution, when Communist workers' councils seized control not only of the entire daily press—except the great Socialist daily *Republica*—but also of the radio and television stations.

These weeklies have managed to avoid the flabby administrative overhead that characterized the pre-junta press, when owner-banks used the losses as a tax write-off. At least two, the conservative *Tempo* and center-left *Expresso*, have been consistent money-makers. One of the best is *O Jornal*, founded in 1975 as an independent leftist paper by Joaquim Letria, a TV personality who had been information director of the state-owned television service. Fed up by censorship from below by the workers' councils, he rallied to his new journals 15 former newsmen who were willing to work unsalaried at the outset. *Jornal* then joined a small housing journal which now owns 48 percent of the paper and provides administrative and advertising support. The paper had 90,000 circulation, immense by Lisbon standards, in its first year and made a profit. Down to 62,000 in late 1977, the paper was in a touch-and-go financial situation, having run at a profit in the first half of the year and at a deficit in the second.

Republica is no longer published. It became a *cause célèbre* in 1975 when printers to the left of the Communists seized the paper in a feud with its Socialist editorial staff. In a move that helped topple the triumvirate, Mário Soares, now the nation's premier, withdrew from that provisional government in protest against its unwillingness to order the paper returned to the Socialists. *Republica* finally was returned in January 1976, but by then its editor, Raul Rego, who had served two terms in prison for his unorthodox views in the Salazar days, had founded a new evening daily, *A Luta* ("The Fight").

The Press and Government Subsidies

The independent press has been arguing for continued and enlarged government subsidies, contending that only state support can maintain a press not dominated either by the political parties or the government itself. The independents already enjoy free postage inside the country, reduced telex and telephone rates and subsidized newsprint.

In a lengthy article on the newspaper situation shortly before the government decision, the editor of *Tempo*, Nuno Rocha, who is also chairman of the International Press Institute in Lisbon, argued that it was imperative that the government take a firm stand in weeding out the state-owned papers and subsidizing the independents. He said the assets of two of the closed newspapers could be sold and that some papers could be merged or turned into cooperatives. One suggestion heard during the year of debate is that the government create an "Institute of State Participation" in which it would retain part of the capital but put management of its interests in the hands of an impartial administrator.

Among contemplated mergers have been the integration of two Oporto papers, *Jornal de Noticias* and *O Comercio do Porto*, into a single morning paper, and the amalgamation of *A Capital*, an evening Lisbon paper, into the government organ, *Diario de Noticias*. *A Capital* is a center-left daily that closely supports the government, but it is an especially big money loser. *Diario* is the circulation leader in the country at 86,000 and the only broadsheet daily. Since the shakeout of Communists that demoted or reassigned 22 staffers, the paper has been reasonably impartial, even in its news coverage of Alvaro Cunhal, the Communist Party chief, although the editorials reflect government thinking.

Opponents of Press Reorganization

Opponents of the press reorganization plans include the unions, protesting the loss of possibly upwards of 3,000 jobs. Editors of the threatened papers also have been vocal. *A Capital's* editors, in an eloquent appeal carried in *O Jornal*, said the paper's continued independent identity was warranted because *A Capital* was committed to objectivity. The press has indeed become more sober and responsible since the early days of the revolution, when it reflected not only the Communist surge but also the general chaos. The government has plans to create a school of journalism to replace *ad hoc* night courses now offered with informal government support. The International Press Institute has pledged as yet unspecified aid to the press under a grant from a Norwegian foundation.

Still other critics of the government's move protest that a cutback in the number of newspapers would signify disrespect for the new constitution because it does not limit or condition the operation of the press. Given the difficulties of operating a newspaper in a stagnant economy, the argument for government aid becomes plausible. However, it has always been clear that a nationalized press and an open dialogue are incompatible in the long run. Portugal's chancy but idealistic search for a better way to achieve "variety in unity" certainly deserves the attention of free people everywhere.

VI. IBERIA AND FOREIGN RELATIONS

EDITOR'S INTRODUCTION

Neither Spain nor Portugal are very active in the foreign policy arena. But their growing interest in the North Atlantic Treaty Organization (NATO), the European Economic Community (EEC), and Portugal's hope for financial aid from the International Monetary Fund (IMF) will undoubtedly change their stance in the future. This section provides previews of what relations the two countries may develop with these international organizations. The topic of Eurocommunism is also discussed, since change in the structures and policies of the Communist parties will have foreign policy implications.

The first article by Joe Gandelman, special correspondent of The Christian Science Monitor, discusses relations between the two countries themselves, which have recently been set on a new course owing to the new regimes. The Spanish debate about NATO is then covered by James M. Markham, special correspondent of the New York *Times*. Following are three articles on the subject of the long road to the EEC for Spain and Portugal, first by Francisco Granell, director of the Barcelona Center for International Economic Studies, and two articles from *The Economist*. Notice is also taken of Portugal and the IMF by Helen Gibson, special correspondent of *The Christian Science Monitor*. Two articles deal with the subject of Eurocommunism: one by Louis B. Fleming, a Los Angeles *Times* staff writer, the other by Lucy Komisar, a writer who interviewed Santiago Carrillo, leader of the Spanish Communist party.

PORTUGAL, SPAIN FORGE NEW TIES [1]

Spain and Portugal have replaced the "Iberian Pact," signed nearly 40 years ago by their countries' former dictators, with a new friendship and cooperation treaty.

Thus, a "special relationship" concluded by dictatorial regimes formally ends, and a new, forward-looking one between two young democracies begins.

Portugal's Premier Mário Soares, who came to Madrid for the signing November 22, [1977] told the Lisbon correspondent of the Spanish daily *ABC*: "I have always thought that it was necessary to revise the Iberian Pact. It had been converted into an obviously obsolete diplomatic instrument with ideological connotations no longer adequate to the two peninsular countries' circumstances."

The Iberian Pact was signed March 17, 1939, by General Franco and Portugal's strong man, Dr. Antonio de Oliveira Salazar, who ruled from 1932-1968. It was a friendship and nonaggression pact designed to protect the countries' regimes by ensuring neither would become a base of attack against the other. Dr. Salazar's Portugal subsequently "lobbied" for Franco Spain's entrance into the United Nations (it entered) and NATO (it did not).

Ripples in one country, it was said, would influence the other. Yet, while both have emerged from dictatorships and are therefore preoccupied over the role of their armies, their approaches and perceptions of each other vary.

Portugal opted in 1974 for a bloodless "revolution," a complete break with the past.

Spain after General Franco's passing two years ago opted for reconciliatory negotiated "change without trauma" embracing all political forces.

The Spanish experiment appears to have produced a more stable democracy. Three things may have made the difference:

[1] Article by Joe Gandelman, special correspondent. *Christian Science Monitor.* p 25. N. 25, '77. Reprinted by permission from *The Christian Science Monitor.*

1. General Franco left Spain a symbol of continuity in King Juan Carlos, who calmed rightists and guided reforms in their early stages. In Portugal, slow-moving "reformist" premier Marcello Caetano, who had succeeded Dr. Salazar, was ousted in the 1974 army coup.

2. Spain had an easier time decolonizing than Portugal did. In Portugal the colonial policy under the dictatorship and the drain on national resources caused by fighting three colonial wars in Africa radicalized the army. By divesting itself of its colonies peacefully Spain deprived its leftists of an issue they might have used to seek support from within the army.

3. Spain's middle class was dismayed at the impact radical change had on the economy in Portugal. It would have had too much to lose in a similar upheaval at home.

One aim of the new Iberian treaty will be to emphasize the two countries' quest to "join Europe." Portugal belongs to NATO, and both seek entrance to the European Community. There is even some speculation that Spain's Premier Adolfo Suárez would like the countries admitted to the EEC at the same time.

SPANIARDS DEBATE ENTERING NATO [2]

Spaniards are debating whether they should join the North Atlantic Treaty Organization, and the outcome of their debate, which will be of considerable importance for both Spain and the Western alliance, is far from certain.

The discussion, conducted largely in political circles and the press, touches the elementary question of Spain's place in Europe—an issue that the last two centuries have left unresolved. Spain remained neutral in both world wars and today the feeling runs strong, particularly among the young, that the nation should chart an independent course.

"The Europeans and the Americans do not understand the reluctance of Spain to enter NATO because they think it is like any other European country," said José Ramón

[2] From "Spaniards Debating Membership in NATO," by James M. Markham, special correspondent. New York *Times*. p 6. My. 7, '78. © 1978 The New York Times Company. Reprinted by permission.

Lasuén, a member of Parliament belonging to the governing Union of the Democratic Center and a foreign policy adviser to Prime Minister Adolfo Suárez. "But it isn't. The dialogue is going to be difficult. There is a slight majority of Spanish opinion in favor of entry, but the willingness to enter is very low."

Both King Juan Carlos and the Prime Minister favor joining NATO, but Mr. Suárez heads a minority government that is facing a grave economic crisis and, at the same time, is guiding a new constitution through Parliament. The NATO question could well turn on the government's ability to retrieve a political momentum that many feel it does not now have.

Leftists Opposed to Joining

The Socialist Workers Party, the second largest grouping in Parliament, and the Communists oppose joining the alliance, asserting that Spain should adopt a neutralist policy and avoid entanglements in big-power rivalries. "The experience that we have witnessed in the last 30 years is that countries that have the least connections to blocs have the greatest margin of maneuver," said Luis Yáñez, the Socialists' foreign affairs expert. "But this doesn't mean that we are anti-Atlanticist."

Curiously, the leftists who oppose membership in NATO have tactical allies among elderly far-right officers in the military establishment, particularly in the 220,000-man army. The army is the least prepared of the three services to enter the alliance and would most likely be reduced in size to increase its quality and mobility if Spain joined. Younger officers tend to favor participation in NATO.

The Franco regime maintained the army as an oversized, badly equipped internal police force and only one paratroop brigade is thought to be of NATO caliber. By contrast, the 48,000-man navy, which interests NATO planners considerably, has for years been conducting maneuvers with the American Sixth Fleet, as well as with French, Italian and Belgian naval forces. The navy is confident of its abilities and knows it stands to grow in a NATO role of patrolling north-south sea lanes in the Atlantic, the Strait of Gibraltar and the Western Mediterranean.

US Has Bases in Spain

The 41,000-man air force, with 157 combat aircraft, has held joint exercises with the United States 16th Air Force, which has the use of four bases in Spain under an agreement that expires in 1981. One political insider said the navy was "150 percent in favor of NATO, the air force 110 percent in favor and the army 60 to 70 percent in favor."

The arguments for Spain's entry, which were put to a group of Spanish legislators at a NATO-approved seminar held in Britain last month, are that it will prompt the modernization of the armed forces, divert officers from political dabbling to purely military questions, give Madrid an important say in the councils of Europe, strengthen the defense of the Canary Islands and make it easier for Britain to hand over Gibraltar, which could become a NATO base under a formula that restores Spanish sovereignty there.

The Spaniards were also told that membership in NATO would cost less than armed neutrality, but Mr. Yáñez, one of three Socialists who attended the discussions, said he was unconvinced on this score. The Socialists also found it offensive that the Communists were excluded from the gathering, which was addressed by General Alexander M. Haig Jr., the NATO commander.

The Soviet Union has been conducting an energetic campaign to dissuade Spaniards from entering NATO. "We do not want Spain to enter NATO," said Viktor G. Afanasyev, editor of *Pravda*, on a recent visit to Madrid. "Spain's joining NATO could prevent the development of Spanish-Soviet relations."

LONG ROAD TO THE EEC [3]

Spain's deep interest in the European Community can be understood when one realizes that today the EEC repre-

[3] Article by Francisco Granell, director of the Barcelona Center for International Economic Studies. *The Banker*. 128:65-70. Ap. '78. © The Financial Times Limited 1978. Reprinted from *The Banker* with the Editor's permission.

sents Spain's major trading partner. In 1977, Spanish imports from the nine members of the Community amounted to $6.1 billions, from a total import bill of $17.9 billions (34.1 percent). Spanish exports to the Community reached $4.8 billions, in a total export bill of $10.3 billions (46.3 percent). Moreover, capital brought in by Community tourists and remittances from Spanish workers in the Community are important in the overall relationship between the Community and Spain as well as for the Spanish balance of payments.

On February 9, 1962, Sr. Castiella, the Spanish Foreign Minister, wrote to M. Couve de Murville, then Chairman of the Council of Ministers of the Six, asking for the opening of negotiations on a permanent link between Spain and the European Community.

The Spanish letter to the EEC reflected in part a fear of being excluded forever from the construction of Europe but in part too was prompted by a survey of Spanish opinion in which the majority of bodies, both public and private, consulted by the government had been in favor of an "opening-up process to Europe." At that time, the Spanish request for association received no more than an acknowledgement from the EEC and several European political leaders barely hid their hostility towards Franco's political régime.

It was only after two EEC mandates (July 7, 1967 and October 17, 1969) and long years of discussions that the chief Spanish negotiator, Sr. Alberto Ullastres, was able to reach a preferential trade agreement with the Six, which was signed by the Spanish Foreign Minister, Sr. Lopez Bravo, in Luxembourg on June 29, 1970.

Under the 1970 EEC-Spanish Agreement, still in force today, dutiable Spanish goods exported to the Six (now the Nine) benefit from reduced Community customs tariffs. The reduction has progressed to 60 percent. Nevertheless, there are certain exceptions: ECSC [European Coal and Steel Community] products are not included and "sensitive" products are on a special list with a maximum tariff reduction of 40 percent. Preferential treatment for Spanish agricultural products was also restricted.

In exchange, Spain undertook to reduce tariffs on dutiable EEC products imported into Spain. These goods were divided into three categories and the last tariff reductions, implemented on January 1, 1977, brought the cumulative reduction to 60 percent, 25 percent and 25 percent respectively for the three categories. Some products were totally excluded from any tariff reduction.

It is very difficult to assess the impact of the 1970 Agreement on relations between Spain and the EEC, because it has been in force during a period marked by considerable international monetary disorder, by the upheaval caused by the enlargement of the Community, and by the oil and commodity crises.

Spain's agreement with the EEC has, therefore, been only one of the factors affecting the recent development of its trade.

Spain was able to increase its exports to the EEC Nine by over 206 percent between 1970 and 1976. But total Spanish exports were also growing rapidly during this period and the EEC's *share* of this total has remained steady. Spain has been responsible for an increasing share of the non-oil imports of the United States, EFTA [European Free Trade Association], and most of the developing countries, and this without any special trade arrangements, and has become increasingly important as a supplier of EEC non-oil imports (it accounted for 2.5 percent of EEC non-oil imports in 1970 and 3.6 percent in 1976).

EEC Threat to Spanish Agriculture

The entry of Denmark, Ireland and the United Kingdom into the European Community on January 1, 1973, created a new situation which could have a serious effect on the traditional flow of Spanish agricultural exports to the United Kingdom. EEC tariffs were much higher than the original British ones. The Community itself recognized this and other problems arising for Spain and agreed to revise the 1970 EEC-Spain Agreement in the context of a global approach aimed also at solving the problems of other Mediterranean countries and Israel.

On June 25, 1973, the EEC Council gave a mandate to the Commission to negotiate in this respect but during the negotiations there were conflicting pressures within the EEC: while businessmen were generally in favor of establishing stronger ties with Spain, parliaments and public opinion were concerned about the political implications of negotiating with the Franco régime.

The negotiations were not completed during Franco's life. At the very last moment, the British government decided unilaterally to apply a "standstill" which was welcomed both by Spanish exporters and by British consumers, since it helped to keep British domestic food prices low.

After Franco's death in November 1975, the first government of King Juan Carlos reconsidered the Spanish position with respect to the Community. An application for full membership of the Community was officially submitted on July 28, 1977, by the Spanish Foreign Minister, Sr. Marcelino Oreja.

Today, in the absence of a new agreement, the 1970 preferential agreement continues to apply but the situation is complex. Spain is reluctant to negotiate a new trade agreement until the question of membership can be discussed. At the same time, the EEC, instead of trying to help Spain by following a generous and open policy, has tried to cut the growth of Spanish exports, by quantitive and administrative measures and by approving a new and restrictive mandate for re-negotiation with Spain (December 20, 1977).

What Full Membership Would Mean for Spain

(a) Legal and institutional adjustments:

It could take eight or nine years of negotiations before Spain becomes a full EEC member. The present EEC members are unable to commit themselves to an exact date for Spain's admission while they are still considering the implications of the negotiations under way with Greece (following its application to join the EEC on June 12, 1975) and Portugal (it applied to join the EEC on February 8, 1977). In terms of economic strength, population and area, Spain is the most important of the would-be members of the Community.

The further enlargement of the Community to 12 members will undoubtedly pose a number of serious problems, affecting the functioning of the Community's institutions as well as its economic, industrial, agricultural and social arrangements. Spanish laws and institutions will also be affected by EEC membership. Adjustment to Community conditions will involve a real revolution in the administrative mechanism of the Spanish state, as well as in the organizational methods of most firms. In order to face all these tasks, a new ministry (without portfolio) was created in February 1978 with Sr. L. Calvo Sotelo as head.

When the moment comes and Spain is accepted into the EEC, the country will obviously have to adopt the Community's legislation and original treaties. This will include adoption of the system of indirect Community taxation (involving the introduction of VAT [value-added tax]). Spain will also have to modify, entirely or in part, its legislation on competition, state trading monopolies, social matters, companies, patents, agricultural policy, trademarks, etc.

(b) The free movement of goods: effects on Spanish agriculture and industry:
    The gradual removal of tariff barriers between Spain and the EEC, the adoption of the Common External Tariff, and the open commercial policy of the Community will expose Spanish exports and domestic production to direct competition from abroad. The economic advantages of integration within the EEC should derive from a stronger competitive position within a large and expanding market, a more efficient allocation of resources, economies of scale and forced changes in efficiency due to increased foreign com-

petition. These developments should in due course induce a higher rate of growth and rising per capita incomes.

The Spanish agricultural sector will be the first to benefit from free trade, price supports and export subsidies under the Community's Common Agricultural Policy. This will result in higher incomes for Spanish farmers, since current prices of several farm products are lower in Spain than in the EEC. Higher EEC farm prices will be an incentive for Spanish farmers to increase their output.

In industry, a great effort will have to be made by industrialists. Spanish businessmen must realize that large financial incentives, excessive protectionism and low labor costs, which in the past ensured fast and comfortable growth, will no longer be available. Small and medium-sized firms in particular will need extensive reorganization and modernization. Firms will now have to pay much more attention to foreign markets than in the past and make an important effort to improve their productivity, marketing and technology.

(c) Free movement of labor and the right of establishment:

Free movement of workers is provided for by the Rome Treaty and member states may no longer (except in the public service) discriminate against citizens of other Community member states by giving priority for a job to one of their own citizens. This means that Spain's entry into the EEC will allow free movement of labor between Spain and all other EEC countries and provide Spanish workers in the Community with more rights than they have now. Several observers have suggested that the labor movement provisions of the Rome Treaty could stimulate an exodus of workers from Spain, Portugal and Greece to the Community because of domestic unemployment problems and because the proportion of the labor force still employed in farming in these countries is higher than in the EEC. Some qualified observers feel that the solution to this potential exodus of workers can be found only through a re-allocation of investment directed towards labor-intensive processes, which implies a shift away from Western and Northern Europe into countries of the Mediterranean area, and through a more active regional policy.

(d) The free movement of capital and banking services:
Progress towards relaxing capital controls within the EEC has in practice been very slow, and the Community's experience suggests that Spain could retain some of its present foreign exchange controls and ease only those controls relating to transactions with EEC countries (mainly by authorizing direct EEC investments and access by EEC subsidiaries in Spain to internal credits).

When Spain joins the community, EEC banks and other financial institutions will be allowed to establish subsidiaries in Spain on the same terms as local banks.

IBERIA AND THE EUROPEAN COMMUNITY [4]

The EEC commission, in a lovingly-painted "fresco" on the impact of enlargement on the Community due to go to the council of ministers later this month [April 1978], leaves no doubt that the present Nine must welcome Greece, Spain and Portugal into the club. The "fresco" has not yet been finalized, but its outlines are now clear. The three countries' applications are based on a political commitment (and, though the commission does not say so, the applicants' faith in the power of membership to keep them on the path of democratic righteousness is both touching and awe-inspiring). So the response, the commission argues, must be political too. After all, the Treaty of Rome asks member countries "to preserve and strengthen peace and liberty," and calls upon "the other peoples of Europe who share their ideal to join in their efforts."

That is not to say that enlargement will not be hard

[4] From "A Picture of a Community." *The Economist*. 267:45 and 48. Ap. 1, '78. © The Economist Newspaper Ltd., London, 1978. Reprinted with permission.

work. On the plus side, the Community can look back on its experience of getting the original Six to move closer to each other and of integrating three new members after the first round of enlargement in 1973. On the minus side, the economic world around it is a much rougher place now than it was at the beginning of 1973, with high unemployment everywhere and protectionism rearing its head all around; and the applicant countries are a lot poorer and less developed than most of the existing members. But the commission insists that enlargement must not mean a dilution of the Community. The *acquis communautaire*—the Community's achievements so far—must be preserved.

Specific problems will crop up in a number of fields, notably agriculture. The applicant countries' farms are on the whole smaller and poorer than the present Community average, and will need a lot of help to catch up. Enlargement will make the Community more self-sufficient, or push it into surplus, in products such as wine and fresh fruit and vegetables. There may be some compensating advantages; the Spanish, for example, point out that they are net importers of meat, milk products and cereals and could relieve the existing Nine of some of their surpluses. But the net effect of enlargement, on any reasonable assumptions, will be more spending on the common farm policy.

Industrial policy too will become more difficult in a Community of 12. Some of the Nine's problem industries, such as steel, textiles and shoes, are precisely those that the applicant countries are now trying to develop in their effort to reduce their dependence on farming. The commission bravely argues that the Nine may have to help them in this, even at the risk of making their own industrial problems temporarily worse. But politicians in present member states may find this kind of magnanimity hard to swallow. They will also look warily at the commission's suggestion that freedom of movement for workers from new member states can be "gradually" introduced as long as enough is done to create jobs for them in their home countries.

The Differing Economic Needs

The economic needs of the three applicant countries differ markedly from each other. The commission believes that Spain or Greece will not need large-scale aid from existing members to prepare them for entry, but is convinced that Portugal will need a lot of support to remedy its structural economic problems and its political instability. A pre-entry phase of adjustment might be one way out, but the commission rejects this and calls for full entry without further delay. The transitional period, during which the new members would be spared the full costs and obligations of membership (though they would fully participate in all institutions), should be at least five years (as for the last batch of entrants), proposes the commission; but not more than 10.

To prevent the Community's institutional machinery from grinding to a halt under the weight of three new members, it will have to be changed, says the commission; but not too radically. All member states should still be represented in every Community institution, which will mean major upheavals as the new members are phased in. But there will have to be greater use of majority voting in the council of ministers, the commission proposes; and (surprise) the commission should be given greater administrative and executive powers.

Relations with the outside world will change too. With Turkey, they are likely to become even more delicate than they are already—thanks to Greek entry. The balance the Nine have tried to achieve in their dealings with the Mediterranean countries as a whole may also be upset, and liberal financial aid may be needed to redress it. The African, Caribbean and Pacific countries, with which the EEC has a special trade and aid pact, will not be much affected, but other developing countries may suffer from enlargement. Against that, the EEC will get new links with Latin America—an area of the world it has always neglected.

THE EEC AND PORTUGAL [5]

Full membership of the EEC could be highly damaging for Portugal's economy, the poorest in western Europe, say many officials in the EEC commission. The commission's official verdict on Portugal's application to join the Community, due to be published in late April [1978], will be less blunt. But it will emphasize the fragility of the Portuguese economy and the need to give Portugal a transition period of a good 10 years before it has to apply all the EEC's rules. Mr. Lorenzo Natali, the EEC commissioner in charge of enlargement, was in Lisbon this week to give the Portuguese a preview.

Portugal officially applied for membership almost exactly a year ago. Its motives—and the motives of the EEC ministers who welcomed the application—were essentially political. The prime minister, Mr. Mário Soares, believes that if Portugal is in the EEC it will be far harder for non-democrats to seize power.

There is a widespread belief in Lisbon, eagerly encouraged by Mr. Soares, that EEC membership will bring economic benefits as well. In his election manifesto Mr. Soares stated that EEC membership would bring "European living standards" to Portugal. That would mean a staggering change. At present Portugal has an income per head of only around $1500, compared with the EEC's average of $5250.

However, the Portuguese economy is so weak that sudden exposure to EEC competition would almost certainly make matters worse. Many of its problems are structural. The majority of its factories are tiny. Of a total of 43,000 firms, a mere 1,100 employ over 100 workers. Next, industry is heavily concentrated in vulnerable sectors. Over 27 percent of Portugal's total exports in 1976 were of textiles and footwear, 21 percent were of farm products (such as port and

[5] From "EEC and Portugal: Is It Worth It?" *The Economist.* 267:48-9. Ap. 1, '78. © The Economist Newspaper Ltd., London, 1978. Reprinted with permission.

tomato concentrates) and 16 percent were of wood and cork. All these products face static or falling world demand. Further, Portugal is busy investing public funds in new industries destined for trouble, such as steel, shipbuilding and petrochemicals.

Portugal will gain some benefits from free access to EEC markets in textiles, having been hit especially hard by the curbs on sales to Britain under the multifibre arrangement. But the gain may be turned into a loss when Portugal has to face the same competition as the Community now faces from countries such as Korea.

Portugal has slender hopes of exporting capital-intensive products such as petrochemicals, steel and cement to the EEC. In more labor-intensive industries it would also find it hard to compete with Asian countries. It might be able to increase exports of certain capital goods such as farm machinery and some machine tools. And several Portuguese economists reckon that Portugal could develop medium-technology industries such as making furniture. But these are crumbs for a famine.

The revolution in Portugal in 1974 brought new problems. Nationalization has proved disruptive enough (although some nationalized industries, such as cement, have managed to achieve high production growth in the past two years)—but the permissive labor legislation has badly dented productivity. Following the land takeovers in southern Portugal, farm production has fallen sharply.

Portugal's Foreign Trade Position

Portugal's foreign trade position is disastrous by any standard. . . . The country's current balance has got progressively worse. Its trade with the EEC is quite lopsided. In the first three quarters of 1977, Portugal exported only half as much to the EEC as it imported from there.

It is hard to see what Portugal can do to right its adverse trade balance. Over 70 percent of its imports are food, materials and capital goods essential for investment. Entry into the EEC would sharply boost Portugal's food import bill. It might also send imports of manufactures soaring.

Portuguese officials angrily deny that the country is now heavily protected by tariff barriers. Tariffs on EEC imports, they say, have been steadily reduced since the 1972 trade agreement was signed. Most tariffs are due to be completely eliminated by 1980; the last batch will go by 1985. But they omit to mention the raft of non-tariff barriers.

According to the Organization for Economic Co-operation and Development, Portugal has an import elasticity of 1.5. This means that for every one percent rise in gross domestic product, imports will rise by $1\frac{1}{2}$ percent. So the country faces two equally unpleasant choices. Either it can deflate sharply and cut growth to reduce the trade deficit, or it continues and perhaps increases its protectionism. Or both?

The International Monetary Fund has strongly argued for the first course. It has persuaded Portugal's new finance minister (and the country's former chief EEC expert), Mr. Vitor Constancio, to raise taxes by a third this year and tighten the credit squeeze. Some deflation is essential in a country where inflation was 27 percent last year. But the IMF's target for a halved trade deficit this year seems unrealistic.

The EEC Response

The most rational EEC response to Portugal's dilemma would be to offer political membership of the EEC but to postpone economic membership. This could be done by allowing Portugal to join the EEC's political co-operation network (as Belgium suggested last year) and perhaps even to attend the thrice-yearly EEC summits. But now that Spain has also applied to join, EEC politicians feel it would be impossible to split Iberia by allowing the Spaniards but not Portugal full membership. Most of them reckon the two should join simultaneously.

PORTUGAL AND THE IMF [6]

After walking off in a huff earlier this month [March 1978], the International Monetary Fund (IMF) is due to return to Lisbon March 29 to resume the negotiations for Portugal's badly needed loans.

The tiff apparently came over the Portuguese Government's refusal to go all the way with the stiff austerity measures demanded by the IMF to counter what is now officially a $1.4 billion balance-of-payments deficit—it was quoted as $1.2 billion recently—for last year. The Portuguese have been told they must cut this by $500 million for the April 78-79 fiscal year.

When the IMF comes back (at the written invitation of the Economic Minister), if all goes well Portugal should get its $50 million IMF loan and see this body unfreeze the loans from 14 countries that make up another $750 million in aid.

But even if Portugal does get the long-awaited funds, Economic Minister Vitor Constancio has made it clear that this is only a temporary stopgap. The obviously strained Mr. Constancio told the American Businessmen's Club recently that if these loans were only intended as a one-shot affair, "then I should be very worried indeed as to the solution of our economic problems."

The foreign and local private businessmen, who packed a ballroom of a Lisbon Hotel, had come in the hope of hearing cheering words about the future. They were not particularly reassured.

Mr. Constancio told them that industrial imports must be reduced by six to seven percent, that prices were expected to rip upward next month, that the credit squeeze planned would prevent firms accumulating stocks, that firms would not be able to expect an increase in unit profit margins. To

[6] From "IMF Ready to Negotiate Again on Portuguese Request for Loans," by Helen Gibson, special correspondent. *Christian Science Monitor.* p 21, Mr. 28, '78. Reprinted by permission from *The Christian Science Monitor.* © 1978 The Christian Science Publishing Society. All rights reserved.

one businessman who asked whether the endless bureaucracy which slowed everything down was not going to be cut to let everyone get on with their jobs, the Minister replied that there were laws that had to be followed.

The Minister said he was aware that increasing exports—over 90 percent of which are produced in Portugal by the private sector—was one of the principal ways of combating the huge external deficit that has been built up. He admitted that to do this businessmen needed confidence in the economic climate and a stimulus to expand and invest. To accomplish this, he again urged the need for outside monetary support and guarantees of future aid. At the moment, he said, Portugal did not have them.

There is more and more reliance on monetary policies and less on real policies, businessman José Morais Cabral said. "We businessmen can't expand because we don't know what lies ahead."

SPAIN AND EUROCOMMUNISM [7]

At a reception given recently by Italy's ambassador to the Vatican, the center of attention was not a cardinal, not an archbishop, but the secretary general of Italy's Communist Party, Enrico Berlinguer.

On a recent evening in Paris, more than 50,000 people turned out for a political rally. The speaker was Georges Marchais, secretary general of the French Communist Party.

And in Madrid, it is no secret that high government officials have consulted regularly with Santiago Carrillo, secretary general of the Spanish Communist Party, in the 11 months since his party was legalized.

There is no question that the leaders of the 2.7 million Communists in Italy, France and Spain are now in the mainstream of their societies.

The three leaders have met only once, a year ago in

[7] From "Three Faces of Eurocommunism—Italy, France and Spain," by Louis B. Fleming, a staff writer. Los Angeles *Times*. p 32 I. F. 26, '78. Copyright 1978. Los Angeles Times. Los Angeles Times/Washington Post News Service. Reprinted with permission.

Madrid. Their purpose then was to bring pressure to bear on the government of Spain to legalize the Communist Party. The following month, the party was legalized, in time to participate in the June election.

But if these three men share some common goals, they are as diverse personally as the parties they lead.

They have two things in common:

Each is the son of a father committed to the correction of social injustice.

And each has come to embrace the concept of Euro-communism, publicly affirming the independence of his party, particularly its independence from Moscow, rejecting the concept of a dictatorship of the proletariat, accepting a commitment to work through democratic parliamentary means to achieve power.

Most of Berlinguer's biographers say that he had a comfortable childhood inspired by a lawyer father committed to a polite form of socialism and to social reform. Even as a child, Berlinguer was quiet and aloof. He was a loner, an avid reader, but a mediocre student.

He came to communism through the youth movement just as fascism was being driven from Italy. The Italian government had surrendered to allied troops. It was 1943, he was 21 years old and he was arrested in connection with demonstrations protesting a crisis in food distribution for the poor.

In succeeding years, Berlinguer advanced rapidly in youth work. He was named secretary general of youth work in 1949 and became president of the world Federation of Democratic Youth the next year. In 1958, he entered the party secretariat in Rome and 10 years later was named deputy secretary general, clearly the heir of aging and ailing Luigi Longo.

His role is depicted as that of a meticulous, quiet mediator, holding the party together under the strains of competing points of view.

"Major decisions are taken on a collegial basis," a Western diplomat expert in party affairs said recently.

"When he is preparing a speech, he is very precise and detailed," said Luciano Barca, one of 36 members of the party directorate. "He wants notes from different people. He asks many questions, he is not easily persuaded. He always wants verification."

That same sort of consultation probably went into Berlinguer's first major policy contribution after taking the direction of the party. That was his articulation of the *compromesso storico*—the Historic Compromise—his proposal that the Left, Communists and Socialists rule jointly with the largest of the Italian parties, the Christian Democrats. The words were first used in 1973. Party policy has not wavered since then.

Like most political leaders in Europe, Berlinguer tries to keep his personal life private. Now 55, he is married and has four children. The fact that the wife of this avowed atheist is a practicing Roman Catholic does not in the least tarnish his political image in an ostensibly Catholic nation.

Privacy is essential to his security at a time of growing political terrorism, which forces him to travel around Rome in a carefully guarded convoy of cars.

The French Communist Party

The French party leader, Marchais, 57, has been a Communist for decades but is a relatively recent convert to Eurocommunism.

Jean Kanapa, foreign affairs director of the French party, has sought to trace the party's independence to prewar years. But most historians date the break with Moscow to 1974, when Soviet Ambassador Stepan Tchervonenko tilted the French presidential election against the Left by making a celebrated election eve call on Valery Giscard d'Estaing.

"The new policies did not really show until 1975," a foreign diplomat in Paris, who follows party affairs closely, recalled.

Marchais had already been secretary general for three years. Indeed, it was not until the party congress of 1976 that there was a formal decision to abandon advocacy of the dictatorship of the proletariat. This late conversion is just one of several factors that stir suspicions about him in some French circles.

There has also been controversy about his actions during the German occupation. According to his official biography, the Germans forced him from his work in a French aeronautics factory in 1942 to the Messerschmitt factory in Germany. But a former high official of the French party said Marchais had volunteered to work in Germany, and Marchais lost an action in the French courts last September when he challenged his accuser. In the trial, Marchais wept as he told the court of being rounded up by German policemen and sent off to Germany, only to escape five months later.

Marchais, the son of a miner and union organizer, joined the Communist Party in 1947. He was already active in union work, and in the succeeding years he moved ahead rapidly in union and party affairs. In 1959 he was named to the party Central Committee and made a member of the political bureau. Two years later, he was made Central Committee secretary in charge of work organization.

There are reports that he played a special role in the 1960s in fighting those who sought to liberalize the party and convert it to the policies it has now come to accept. Whatever he did, he seems to have won the favor of Maurice Thorez and Emile Waldeck-Rochet, the secretaries general with whom he served. In 1970 he was named deputy secretary general, and two years later, secretary general.

Marchais, a man of rough-cut good looks, is not subtle, preferring harsh words and strong actions.

The year of 1972 was critical in the history of the French Left. The Communist Party, then the largest of the leftist parties, signed a common program with the Socialist Party. It was an elaborate statement of where France should go in terms of economic reorganization and direction.

The next year, under the leadership of François Mitterrand, the Socialists overtook the Communists to become the dominant party of the Left. But cooperation survived, and

Communists worked hard to support Mitterrand's bid for the presidency in 1974. The Left lost by one percentage point.

That unity has vanished in this year's national elections, and Marchais has behaved as if he would rather not see the Left in power unless the Communists are assured a more influential role that their votes are likely to earn them.

These maneuvers have raised two fresh suspicions. There has been speculation that Marchais might have bowed to Soviet pressure to break up the possibility of a government of the Left, which, these critics theorize, is not now wanted by Moscow. Others have speculated that this may only be evidence of how unenthusiastic Marchais is about anything short of total Communist control.

"Perhaps it is only a clever election strategy to reinforce the Communist vote in the first round and then he would be in a stronger position to work with the Socialists afterward," one expert said.

The Spanish Communist Party

Carrillo, 63, has the greatest problems of the three. In the last elections, the Italian party received 34 percent of the votes and the French 21 percent. The Spanish party received only 9 percent. Coming out into the open after 40 years of underground activity is not easy. And for most of those 40 years, Carrillo was in exile himself.

He grew up in poverty, according to his own account. He remembers going to worker demonstrations with his father at the age of five. His father, a mine worker, went on to high office in the Republican government of Spain.

Carrillo ended his formal education at 13. He became active in Socialist youth activities, was head of the organization by the time he was 19 years old, and two years later joined the Communist Party.

There is controversy about some of his activities in those years as the Spanish Civil War was coming to an end. He reportedly proposed a policy of moderation on the Left to try to consolidate all anti-fascist forces. But he has been accused of later methodically destroying all non-Communists on the Left. He has also been accused of killing a group of army officer prisoners under his control, but he has admitted only to giving the order to transfer the group. It was during the transfer that they were killed.

Within the clandestine party, operating in exile, he succeeded Dolores Ibarruri as secretary general in 1960. She was in exile in the Soviet Union, he in France. It was the beginning of a turbulent decade for the party.

In 1964 Jorge Semprun and Fernando Claudin were purged for advocating a party line much like the line now embraced by Carrillo. Semprun's book, *The Autobiography of Federico Sanchez*, is a best-seller in Spain today, intensely embarrassing to Carrillo, for it asserts that he has never fully broken his Stalinist ties.

Four years after that party purge, Carrillo attracted world attention with his outspoken criticism of the Soviet invasion of Czechoslovakia. He had just weathered a further split in the party, the withdrawal of a Maoist group, and his statements on Prague brought a further split with a hardline Stalinist group.

The image of Carrillo today is of a smiling, benign grandfather gently nudging his homeland along the path of democracy. But his compliance with the government, openly challenged by Semprun, will be tested at the party congress in April.

SANTIAGO CARRILLO'S VIEWS [8]

Komisar: When did you begin to change your attitude toward the Soviet Union?

Carrillo: That was a long process that began particularly at the time of the 20th Congress of the Communist Party of the Soviet Union when Khrushchev gave his famous report. I realized that, without my knowing it, many things I had

    [8] From "Santiago Carrillo: His Words and U.S. Visit," by Lucy Komisar, a writer. The New York *Times.* p 31. N. 2, '77. © 1977 The New York Times Company. Reprinted by permission.

been saying for many years were not true and that it was necessary to have a more critical and independent attitude and to have our own policy.

Question: What process occurred inside the party to allow discussion of those questions and to change the party line?

Answer: It was a long process and went through various different phases. The process began because for many years we have always made changes in our policy without depending on any foreign party, and inspired by our own vision. There were events that helped us see more clearly—for example, the condemnation of Yugoslavia and afterwards the rectification. Another very negative experience that convinced us that we had to have our own positions—a decisive, key event—was, without a doubt, the invasion of Czechoslovakia, which caused us to state publicly our opposition to the methods and procedures of the Soviets. All that started a discussion inside the party that has progressed and led to this collective adoption of the positions we have today and that are summed up in that fashionable word, Eurocommunism.

Q.: You write in your book [*Eurocommunism and the State*] of Communist Parties that have destroyed political liberty. Which parties are they?

A.: The same Soviet Union and other countries that have followed its model. I think that in those countries democratic liberty, political freedom, today are very reduced and almost nonexistent.

Q.: Does the Soviet Union have a dictatorship of the proletariat?

A.: I think not. I think that what exists in the Soviet Union is not a proletarian dictatorship; it is the Government of a stratum of leaders. A proletarian dictatorship would be a workers' democracy, and I don't believe that exists there today.

Q.: If, as you write, the state is the instrument of the hegemony of one class over another, what do you call the class that has power in the Soviet Union?

A.: I don't think it's a class that has power in the Soviet Union. I think that the Soviet state is a transition state. It is no longer a capitalist state and it is not yet a workers' democracy. It is a transition state in which a stratum of leaders has the power.

Q.: If the Communist Party had power, would you say, "O.K., you don't want us anymore, so we're going"?

A.: Evidently. If the Communist Party had power and the electorate voted against it, the Communist Party would have to leave power. However, I believe that at this time, at least in Spain, that possibility is quite remote.

Are Spanish Communists Democratic?

Q.: Does the Spanish Communist Party function through democratic centralism or through a system of internal democracy?

A.: The Spanish Communist Party functions through democratic centralism. There are many ways of understanding democratic centralism. It can be understood as pure centralism or as a democratic system. We are now preparing some statutes for our next congress that will guarantee the democratic functioning of the party.

Q.: What system do you have for choosing the leaders and the policies of the party?

A.: We are going to establish the secret ballot in the party, and the policy of the party is going to be decided by the congresses in a democratic way. The leaders will also be elected.

Q.: What is the chief difference between Eurocommunists and Socialists?

A.: In truth, I think there is no great difference between a Eurocommunist and a Marxist Socialist. A Communist and a Marxist Socialist are very similar. Now, if you ask me the difference between the Eurocommunists and the Social Democrats, that has an easy answer. The social democracy administers capitalist society, and we propose to transform it.

Q.: How can the convergence of Socialists and Euro-communists come about?

A.: The convergence will occur as the Communists value democracy more and as the Socialists are more Socialist.

Q.: What do you mean—"as the Socialists are more Socialist"?

A.: That means that instead of administering capitalist society, they decide to transform it.

Eurocommunism and the U.S.

Q.: One might think that Eurocommunism was in the interest of the United States as it diminishes the international power of the Soviet Union and provides a model for the countries of Eastern Europe. You say that Kissinger, and I assume you include other American leaders, are against the success of Eurocommunism. Why?

A.: Eurocommunism represents the possibility of the development of forms of Socialism totally independent of the Soviet Union that do not mean the strengthening of the Soviet Union as a power. In that sense, I think it is to the advantage of all of humanity. At the same time, I have to say with all sincerity that Eurocommunism does not mean the strengthening of the power of the United States, either. We do not oppose being an instrument of the Soviet Union in order to become an instrument of the United States, not at all.

Q.: Do you think Spain ought to be in NATO?

A.: No. It is not in NATO now, and I think it is better for Spain to be a nonaligned country.

Q.: Is there a possibility of having in Spain the kind of alliance of Communists and Socialists that exists in France? [This was asked when the collapse of the French Union of the Left did not appear so certain.]

A.: At this time in Spain, there is another problem—to stabilize the democracy that is still very fragile. That is not the task only of Socialists and Communists. It is the task of all the democratic parties, including the bourgeois parties.

BIBLIOGRAPHY

An asterisk (*) preceding a reference indicates that the article or part of it has been reprinted in this book.

BOOKS AND PAMPHLETS

Alba, Victor. Transition in Spain. Transaction Books. '78.

Amodia, Jose. Franco's political legacy: from dictatorship to facade democracy. Rowman and Littlefield. '77.

Bender, G. J. Angola under the Portuguese. Heinemann Educational. '78.

Bookchin, Murray. The Spanish anarchists: 1868–1936. Free Life Editions. '76.

Brandes, S. H. Migration, kinship, and community: tradition and transition in a Spanish village. Academic Press. '75.

Carrillo, Santiago. Eurocommunism and the state. Whirlwind. '78.
  Reviews: In These Times. 2:17. Ja. 25-31, '78. "Eurocommunism" and the state. Hugh Delacy; New Society. 42:531-2. D. 8, '78. Acceptable face. Paul Preston.

Carrillo, Santiago. Problems of socialism today. Beekman Pubs. '70.

Christopher, Peter. Images of Spain. Norton. '77.

Coverdale, J. F. The political transformation of post-Franco Spain. Praeger. '78.

Dolgoff, Sam, ed. The anarchist collectives: Workers' self-management in the Spanish revolution. Free Life Editions. '74.

Feld, W. J., ed. The foreign policies of West European Socialist parties. Praeger. '78.

Fields, R. M. The Portuguese revolution and the armed forces movement. Praeger. '76.

Gallagher, Charles F. Reflections on the Spanish elections. (West Europe Series, v 12, no 2) American Field Staff Inc. 4 West Wheelock St. Hanover, N.H. 03755. '77.

Gallagher, Charles F. Culture and education in Spain. (West Europe Series, v 12, no 3) American Field Staff Inc. 4 West Wheelock St. Hanover, N.H. 03755. '77.

Hansen, E. C. Rural Catalonia under the Franco regime. Cambridge University Press. '77.

Kaplan, Temma. Anarchists of Andalusia, 1868–1903. Princeton University Press. '77.

Kay, Hugh. Salazar and modern Portugal. Hawthorn Books. '70.

Kern, R. W. Red years/black years: a political history of Spanish anarchism, 1911–1937. Institute for the Study of Human Issues. '78.

Laure, Jason and Ettagale. Jovem Portugal: after the revolution. Farrar. '77.

Laxalt, Robert. In a hundred graves: a Basque portrait. University of Nevada Press. '72.

Lowe, Alfonso. The culture and history of the Spanish. Gordon & Cremonesi. '77.

Lowe, Alphonso. The Spanish. Atheneum. '76.

Mailer, Phil. Portugal: the impossible revolution? Free Life Editions. '77.

Marques, A. H. R. de Oliveira. History of Portugal. 2 vols. Columbia University Press. '72.

Maxwell, Kenneth. Revolution in Portugal and Angola. Viking. Early '79.

Michener, James. Iberia: Spanish travels and reflections. Random. '68.

Moore, Kenneth. Those of the street: the Catholic Jews of Mallorca. University of Notre Dame Press. '76.

Payne, S. G. Basque nationalism. University of Nevada Press. '75.

Payne, S. G. A history of Spain and Portugal. University of Wisconsin Press. '76. 2 v.

Payne, S. G., ed. Politics and society in twentieth-century Spain. Franklin Watts. '78.

Poulantzas, Nicos. The crisis of the dictatorships: Portugal, Greece, Spain. Humanities Press. '76.

Preston, Paul, ed. Spain in crisis: the evolution and decline of the Franco regime. Barnes and Noble. '76.

Salisbury, W. T. and J. D. Theberge, eds. Spain in the 1970's. Praeger. '76.

Toynbee, Philip, ed. The distant drum: reflections on the Spanish civil war. David McKay. '77.

Wiarda, H. J. Corporatism and development: the Portuguese experience. University of Massachusetts Press. '77.

Yglesias, José. The Franco years. Bobbs-Merrill. '77.

Periodicals

American Journal of Sociology. 83:386-402. S. '77. Affluence, class structure, and working-class consciousness in modern Spain. J. R. Logan.

Américas. 30:41-5. F. '78. Federico de Onís: paladin of Hispanic culture. Sally Ortiz Aponte.

*Banker (London). 128:35-7. Mr. '78. Portugal: victim of dogma. Basil Caplan.

*Banker (London). 128:57-65. Ap. '78. Spain: the new wind of realism. Joaquin Muns.

*Banker (London). 128:65-70. Ap. '78. Long road to the EEC. Francisco Granell.

Banker (London). 128:70-2. Ap. '78. Catalonia's underlying strength. Andreu Gispert.

Business Week. p 40-1. Ja. 23, '78. Crimp on credit threatens recovery.

Business Week. p 34-6. Ja. 30, '78. Political impasse over oil distribution; Compañia Arrendataria del Monopolio de Petroleos.

Business Week. p 47+. Ap. 10, '78. Spain: businessmen force a cabinet shakeup.

Christian Century. 94:615. Jl. 6, '77. Spain strides toward democracy. T. S. Goslin.

*Christian Science Monitor. p 20. N. 22, '77. Spain's troubled isles. Joe Gandelman.

*Christian Science Monitor. p 25. N. 25, '77. Portugal, Spain forge new ties. Joe Gandelman.

*Christian Science Monitor. p 16. D. 14, '77. Democracy takes root in Spain's countryside. D. D. Gregory.

Christian Science Monitor. p 5. D. 27. '77. Spain, Algeria at odds over Canary Islands. Joe Gandelman.

Christian Science Monitor. p 6. Ja. 3, '78. Spain grants autonomy to Basques. Joe Gandelman.

Christian Science Monitor. p 31. F. 27, '78. Spain's thirst for democratic ideas. Constantine Menges.

Christian Science Monitor. p 6. Mr. 14, '78. Portugal slides toward a brink. Helen Gibson.

*Christian Science Monitor. p 5. Mr. 20, '78. Portuguese in sharp swing toward the right. Helen Gibson.

Christian Science Monitor. p 13. Mr. 22, '78. Cry against A-power picks up in Spain. Joe Gandelman.

*Christian Science Monitor. p 21. Mr. 28, '78. IMF ready to negotiate again on Portuguese request for loans. Helen Gibson.

Christian Science Monitor. p 5. Mr. 29, '78. Eurocommunism's momentum runs down. Eric Bourne.

Christian Science Monitor. p 13. Ap. 18, '78. Azores separatists stir new tensions with Lisbon. Helen Gibson.

Christian Science Monitor. p 14. Ap. 24, '78. Spanish Communists "redefine party." Joe Gandelman.

Christian Science Monitor. p 11. My. 2, '78. Four years after the coup—the Portuguese dream has faded. Helen Gibson.

Christian Science Monitor. p 17. My. 3, '78. Spanish Socialists gaining ground. Joe Gandelman.

*Christian Science Monitor. p 4. My. 5, '78. Portugal's Roman Catholic church uneasy over new civil laws. Helen Gibson.

Christian Science Monitor. p 5. My. 11, '78. Madrid Socialist leader drops a bombshell. Joe Gandelman.

Christian Science Monitor. p 6. Jl. 18, '78. Spain shapes new police image. Joe Gandelman.

*Current History. 73:165-8+. N. '77. The political transformation of Spain. S. G. Payne.

*Current History. 73:169-73+. N. '77. Portugal's crisis. G. W. Grayson.

Dissent. p 338-48. Fall '76. Spain on the eve. Lewis Coser.

Dissent. p 26-42. Winter '78. Eurocommunism—myth, hope, delusion? Irving Howe et al.

Economist (London) . 265:14-15. D. 17, '77. Bring in the centre.

Economist (London) . 265:51-2. D. 17, '77. Spain: birth pangs of a constitution.

Economist (London). 266:73. Ja. 7, '78. Portugal: too little help from its friends.

Economist (London). 267:49. Mr. 4, '78. Whose paws on the Azores?

*Economist (London). 267:45 and 48. Ap. 1, '78. A picture of a community.

Economist (London). 267: 48-9. Ap. 1, '78. EEC and Portugal: Is it worth it?

*Economist (London). 267:69. Ap. 22, '78. We never had it so bad.

Economist (London). 267:16. My. 6, '78. A Schmidt, not a Mitterrand?

Economist (London). 267:58-9. My. 13, '78. A party called Suárez.

Encore. 6:21-4. D. 12, '77. Democracy's growing pains in Spain. David Gardner.

Foreign Affairs. 54:250-70. Ja. '76. The thorns of the Portuguese revolution. Kenneth Maxwell.

Foreign Affairs. 56:190-208. O. '77. Spain's new democracy. Stanley Meisler.

*Harper's. 256:23-9. F. '78. Spain's year of wonders. John Midgley.

In These Times. 2:10. F. 15-21, '78. Spanish women suffer setbacks. Amy Schwartz.

In These Times. 2:9. My. 10-16, '78. Legalized unions launch strike wave. B. M. Franck.

*Inquiry. 1:13-17. My. 1, '78. New day for Catalonia. D. H. Rosenthal.

International Affairs (London). 53:615-30. O. '77. Spain from dictatorship to democracy. J. F. Coverdale.

International Perspectives (Canada). 35-40. S./O. '77. Apprenticeship in democracy with Spain's "civilized" right. J. P. Thouez.

Los Angeles Times. p 2 IV. O. 30, '77. Spain's Carrillo makes red respectable. Stanley Meisler.

Los Angeles Times. p 1 VII. D. 4, '77. A Spanish enclave in Africa. Frank Riley.

*Los Angeles Times. p 2 IV. D. 4, '77. Democracy in Spain is strangely—and ominously—undemocratic. Stanley Meisler.

Los Angeles Times. p 2 VII. Ja. 1, '78. Crisis-ridden Portugal turns once again to Soares. Stanley Meisler.

*Los Angeles Times. p 2 IV. F. 5, '78. Like Spain, its church must change—or perish. M. L. Wolin.

Los Angeles Times. p 1, 1-A-1 IV. F. 19, '78. Anti-semitic scars remain on Majorca. Stanley Meisler.

*Los Angeles Times. p 32 I. F. 26, '78. Three faces of Eurocommunism—Italy, France and Spain. L. B. Fleming.

*Los Angeles Times. p 6 V. Ap. 9, '78. Spain's abused Basques are bitter. Stanley Meisler.

*Los Angeles Times. p 1 IV and 4 IV. Ap. 16, '78. Andalusian unemployment stirs unrest. Stanley Meisler.

Los Angeles Times. p 2 IV. Ap. 30, '78. Spain's ambitious Communists suddenly discover democracy. Stanley Meisler.

Los Angeles Times. p 2 IV. Jl. 9, '78. Spain comes face to face with its troubled history. Stanley Meisler.

Nation. 226: 724-7. Je. 17, '78. How democratic is Spain. Stanley Meisler.

National Geographic. 153:296-331. Mr. '78. Spain. P. T. White.

New America. 15:6-7. Ap. '78. Carrillo's dubious past and the questionable future of Spain's Communist party. Gerald Parsh.

New Leader. 61:4-6. Ja. 30, '78. Wooing Spain's workers: battle between Communists and Socialists. Constantine Menges.

New Leader. 61:13. Je. 5, '78. Canary Islands. Ray Alan.

New Politics. 12:47-52. Winter '78. A new political era in Spain. Wilebaldo Solano.

New Republic. 177:25-7. D. 24 and 31. '77. Spain is coming into her own: Aleixandre's Nobel Prize. Allen Josephs.

*New York Times. p 29. Ja. 30, '76. Spanish refugees: waiting. Nancy Macdonald.

New York Times. p 33. N. 14, '77. Spaniards, a little late, discover Picasso. J. M. Markham.

*New York Times. p 31. N. 23, '77. Santiago Carrillo: his words and U.S. visit. Lucy Komisar.

New York Times. p 2E. D. 4, '77. Portuguese model is something to avoid. J. M. Markham.

*New York Times. p A 7. D. 16, '77. Spaniards shaken by regional unrest. J. M. Markham.

*New York Times. p 16. D. 18, '77. Soaring urban crime troubling Spaniards. J. M. Markham.

New York Times. p 1 and 5. Ja. 1, '78. Basque home rule approved in Spain. J. M. Markham.

New York Times. p 2. F. 7, '78. Spain's Andalusians, beset by
    nomic problems, near autonomy.
*New York Times. p 37. Mr. 8, '78. Troubled Portugal. Ken
    Maxwell.
*New York Times. p 1A and 8A. Mr. 10, '78. Spain, wit
    economy in crisis, finds itself torn politically, too. J.
    Markham.
*New York Times. p 2A. Mr. 29, '78. Flight to cities em
    Spain's countryside. J. M. Markham.
New York Times. p 3. Ap. 9, 78. Catalan defection opens ri
    Spanish Communist ranks. J. M. Markham.
New York Times. p 3F. Ap. 16, '78. The Spanish way of busi
    a tale of three companies. J. M. Markham.
New York Times. p 3E. Ap. 23, '78. In democracy, if West Eu
    gets a 10, Spain gets an 8. J. M. Markham.
New York Times. p 2. Ap. 25, '78. After 300 years, inquisition
    taints some Majorcans. J. M. Markham.
New York Times. p 3A. Ap. 28, '78. Spain's uncommon Cor
    nists: they experiment with democracy. J. M. Markham
*New York Times. p 6. My. 7, '78. Spaniards debating me
    ship in NATO. J. M. Markham.
*New York Times. p 61 & 72. My. 11, '78. A Western bu
    paying income tax, looms in Spain. J. M. Markham.
New York Times. p A2. Je. 16, '78. Spain seems to look to you
    generation for leaders. J. M. Markham.
New York Times. p 2. Jl. 15, '78. Basque disorders point up Sp
    biggest long-term political problem. Jonathan Kandell
New York Times. p A8. Jl. 28, '78. Portuguese governmen
    lapses after president dismisses premier.
New York Times. p A3. Ag. 7, '78. Portugal leader's dea
    passes for forming a governing coalition. Paul Lewis.
New York Times. p A6. Ag. 8, '78. Portuguese revolution: tat
    slogans, a threadbare economy. Paul Lewis.
New York Times Magazine. p 16-17+. O. 3, '76. Spain open
    David Holden.
New York Times Magazine. p 44-5+. D. 4, '77. Homage to
    lona. Anthony Burgess.
New Yorker. 52:41-8+. Mr. 8; 52:103+. N. 29, '76. Our far
    correspondents. Alastair Reid.
Newsweek. p 47. Ag. 7, '78. The sacking of Soares.
*Nieman Reports. 31:55-6. Summer/Autumn '77. Portugal's
    at a crossroads. Milton Hollstein.
Observer (London). p 15. Ap. 9, '78. Eurocommunists start to
    up the pieces. Mark Frankland.
rver (London). p 6. Ap. 16, '78. Portugal gets the bi
    volution years. Robin Smyth.

Orbis. 19:335-78. Summer '75. Portugal and the armed forces movement. G. W. Grayson.

Partisan Review. 45:120-3. N. 1, '78. The consensus in favor of democracy in Spain. Jorge Edwards.

Policy Review. 1:7-26. Summer '77. The specter of Eurocommunism. Robert Moss.

Progressive. 42:20-1. My. '78. On the Spanish civil war. R. A. Rosenstone.

Publishers Weekly. 213:29-35. My. 8, '78. Publishing in Portugal. H. R. Lottman.

Publishers Weekly. 213:37-48+. Je. 12, '78. Publishing in Spain. H. R. Lottman.

Saturday Evening Post. 249:68-9. N. '77. España—Littorally Yours. Carol Schwalberg.

Saturday Evening Post. 249:70-1. N. '77. Portugal: poet kings and the sea. Willis Barnstone.

*Saturday Review. 5:10-20. O. 29, '77. Democracy in Spain: can the impossible dream come true? Horace Sutton.

Saturday Review, 5:22. O. 29, '77. Meanwhile in Portugal . . . Derwent May.

Saturday Review. 5:30-5. O. 29, '77. Iberian islands. Jean Anderson, Marion Gough and Edward McGhee.

Seven Days. 2:20-1. F. 24, '78. Bending over backward. Carlos de Sa Rego.

Swiss Review of World Affairs. 27:6-8. N. '77. Political and economic problems in Spain: growing pains of a democracy. Arnold Hottinger.

*Swiss Review of World Affairs. 27:8-10. N. '77. Alarm in the Spanish economy. Walter Günthardt.

*Swiss Review of World Affairs. 27:19-23. D. '77. Spanish culture in this century. Arnold Hottinger.

Time. 111:45 Ja. 30, '78. Portugal: an odd but hopeful coupling.

Time. 111:32 and 35. My. 1, '78. Spain: democracy v. authority.

Time. 112:34. Jl. 24, '78. Pamplona: the bulls didn't run; rioting by Basque nationalists.

Time. 112:29. Ag. 21, '78. The technocrat; a surprise choice as premier.

*Wall Street Journal. p 34. Ja. 13. '78. Portuguese businessmen back on the job as the government returns their firms. Philip Revzin.

Washington Post. p A24. Ag. 10, '78. Portuguese president appoints industrialist to form government.

Washington Post. p A18. Ag. 21, '78. Political crisis continues in Portugal as left questions choice of Da Costa. Jimmy Burns.

Washington Post. p A16. Ag. 30, '78. Spanish leftists claim killings.

Washington Post. p A9. S. 12, '78. Portugal's government.

087126

Washington Post. p A22. S. 15, '78. Portugal's government toppled
   after 17 days.
*Working Papers for a New Society. 6:20-4. Ja./F. '78. The
   Spanish left: divided but surprisingly strong. Temma Kaplan
   and Jon Wiener.
World Today. 33:358-62. S. '77. Spain on the road to democracy.
   Arnold Hottinger.
*Worldview. 21:14-18. Ap. '78. Deepening shadows over a fragile
   democracy. C. C. Menges.
Yale Review. 67:321-37. Mr. '78. Eurocommunism. Roy Macridis.